TOP 10 WITHDRAWN
ATHENS

Top 10 Athens Highlights

The Top 10 of Everything

CONTENTS

Athens Area by Area

Streetsmart

Within each Top 10 list in this book, no hierarchy of quality or popularity is implied. All 10 are, in the editor's opinion, of roughly equal merit.

Title page, front cover and spine The stunning Parthenon at the Acropolis
Back cover, clockwise from top left Greek salad; The National Observatory; Harbour at Plaka; The Parthenon, Acropolis; Mikromilano, Piraeus

Welcome to
Athens

Ancient temples. World-class museums. Mediterranean sunshine and deep-blue skies. Sandy beaches and waterside nightclubs. Athens brings together the best of ancient and contemporary Greece. It is dynamic, hedonistic and exhilarating, and with Eyewitness Top 10 Athens, it's yours to explore.

We each have our own image of the magnificent **Parthenon** upon the **Acropolis**: an ancient temple in a modern European capital. But it's not until you arrive in Athens that you realize how seamlessly the Ancient Greek monuments and ruins are integrated into Athens' contemporary urban life. Marble columns and beautifully carved pediments lie scattered in an Arcadian meadow next to a busy metro station – this is the **Agora**, at Thisio. The **National Archaeological Museum**, a proud Neo-Classical building, is filled with hoards of invaluable centuries-old treasures next to a street where walls are spray-painted with political slogans, on the edge of Exárhia. But Athens relishes these parallel worlds, and nothing is forbidden.

The city sprawls in a wide valley, protected by rugged mountains, and opening to the south onto the glistening Aegean Sea. From the dense conglomeration of concrete apartment blocks rise two peaks: the aforementioned Acropolis and **Lykavittos Hill**, a rocky mound capped by a tiny church, which is enchantingly floodlit at night. And it is after dark that the city celebrates its passions for eating, drinking and flirting with life.

Whether you are visiting for a weekend or a week, our Top 10 guide brings together the best of everything the city has to offer from the historical **Philopappos Hill** to the stately **Temple of Olympian Zeus**. The guide has useful tips throughout, from seeking out what's free to avoiding the crowds, plus nine easy-to-follow itineraries, designed to tie together a clutch of sights in a short space of time. Add inspiring photography and detailed maps, and you've got the essential pocket-sized travel companion. **Enjoy the book, and enjoy Athens.**

Clockwise from top: **Odeon of Herodes Atticus; Osios Loukas mosaic, Delphi; Brettos, Plaka; Acropolis; Fresco in Kesariani Monastery; Olympic Stadium; National Archaeological Museum**

Exploring Athens

Athens offers a vast range of things to do and see, both ancient and modern. Here are some ideas of how to make the most of your time. The city centre is relatively compact, so you should be able to do most of your sightseeing on foot, without resorting to public transport.

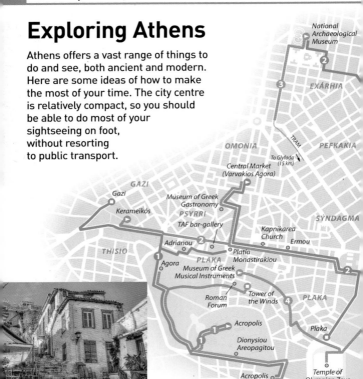

Colourful Plaka is the place to shop for traditional souvenirs.

Two Days in Athens

Day ❶
MORNING
Begin with Athens' centrepiece, the **Acropolis** (see pp12–13), crowned by the Parthenon. See finds from the site at the ultra-modern **Acropolis Museum** (see pp14–15), then lunch at the museum café.

AFTERNOON
Follow the **Dionysiou Areopagitou walkway** (see p60) around the Acropolis to the **Agora** (see pp16–19). Walk to **Platia Monastirakiou** (see p86), stopping in at **Benali Museum of Islamic Art** (see p88) for great textiles, then hunt for souvenirs in **Plaka** (see p79).

EVENING
Dine on contemporary Greek fare in the hip **Gazi** (see p90) neighbourhood.

Day ❷
MORNING
Look in the colourful **Central Market** (see p94; closed Sun), then visit the **Museum of Greek Gastronomy** (see p88; closed Mon). Walk up Ermou, stopping at **Kapnikarea** church (see p87), to Syndagma, home to the **Parliament** (see p101). Walk through the **National Gardens** (see p101) to the **Benaki Museum** (see pp26–7; closed Mon–Tue). Lunch in Kolonaki.

AFTERNOON
Walk, or take the cable car, up **Lykavittos Hill** (see p102) for fabulous

The Parthenon sits atop the Acropolis hill, overlooking Athens.

Key

━━ Two-day itinerary

━━ Four-day itinerary

city views, then cross Exarheia to arrive at the **National Archaeological Museum** (see pp20–21).

EVENING

After an aperitif at the **TAF** bar-gallery (see p82), have dinner in Plaka, below the floodlit Acropolis.

Four Days in Athens

Day ❶

MORNING

Begin with the **Acropolis** (see pp12–13), followed by the ultra-modern **Acropolis Museum** (see pp14–15).

AFTERNOON

Proceed to the **Agora** (see pp16–19) for more ancient history, then explore the cafés and souvenir shops in pretty **Plaka** (see p79), also checking out the Roman Forum **and Tower of the Winds** (see pp24–5).

Day ❷

MORNING

See the **Kerameikos** (see pp30–31) archaeological site, then wander through the colourful **Central Market** (see p94; closed Sun). Walk up Ermou, stopping at the church of **Kapnikarea** (see p87), then proceed to Kolonaki.

AFTERNOON

Visit the **Byzantine and Christian Museum** (see pp32–3). Browse the shops in Kolonaki, refuel with coffee, then check out the nearby **Museum of Cycladic Art** (see pp22–3; closed Tue).

Day ❸

MORNING

Visit the **National Archaeological Museum** (see pp20–21).

AFTERNOON

Catch the tram to **Glyfada** (see p129) and relax on the beach. If it's too cold to swim, head for the thermal waters of **Lake Vouliagmeni** (see p129).

Day ❹

MORNING

Visit the **Museum of Greek Musical Instruments** (see p78; closed Mon) in Plaka. Explore **Philopappos Hill** (see pp34–5) and the **Temple of Olympian Zeus** (see pp36–7), then walk through the **National Gardens** (see p101) to Kolonaki.

AFTERNOON

Visit the **Benaki Museum** (see pp26–7; closed Mon–Tue). Hike up **Lykavittos Hill** (see p102) for views over the city.

Top 10 Athens Highlights

The Parthenon, on the Acropolis

Athens Highlights

Athens is both the Classical, marble-pillared cradle of Western civilization and a modern urban sprawl of concrete and traffic. Between these extremes lies a vibrant city, where the influences of East and West entwine in the markets, cafés and tavernas, which are built upon ancient ruins and rub shoulders with multi-domed Byzantine churches.

Acropolis ➊
The crown jewel of Greece, if not all of Europe. Its temples are among the most influential buildings in Western architecture *(see pp12–15)*.

➋ The Agora
The likes of Socrates, Aristotle and St Paul all held forth in the marketplace below the Acropolis. This was the heart of the ancient city *(see pp16–19)*.

➌ National Archaeological Museum
Finds from some of the world's greatest cultures are housed here. Exhibits include the gold treasure of Mycenae and the first sculptures to depict the complexity of the human form *(see pp20–21)*.

➍ Museum of Cycladic Art
This museum houses one of the largest collections of Cycladic art in the world, showcasing early Bronze Age female marble statuettes which still inspire artists of the modern world *(see pp22–3)*.

➎ Roman Forum and Tower of the Winds
The Romans abandoned the ancient Agora and created this orderly new commercial centre. Its showpiece was the magnificent Tower of the Winds *(see pp24–5)*.

IPEIROU
LIOSION
ACHARNON
VATHIS
PLATIA VATHIS
MARNI
3 SEPTEMVRIOU
MARNI
KAROLOU
ÁGIOS KONSTANDÍNOS
PLATIA OMONIA
OMONIA
PLATIA KOTZIA
(PIREOS)
SOFOKLEOUS
EOLOU
GAZI
TSALDARI
PLATIA ELEFTHERIAS
EVRIPIDOU
IERA ODOS
PANAGI
AG. ASOMATON
DIPILOU
PLATIA IROON
ATHINAS
EOLOU
ERMOU
➐
PSYRRI
ERMOU
ERMOU
PLATIA AVISSYNIAS
PLATIA MONASTIRAKIOU
➋
MONASTIRAKIOU
➎
APOSTOLOU
ASYRMATOS
PAVLOU
Areopagos Rock
ANAFIOTIKA
➊
Hill of the Nymphs
DIONYSIOU
AREOPAGITOU
➒
MAKRYGIANNI
VEIKOU

Benaki Museum **6**

This first-rate collection of Greek art from Neolithic times to the present is housed in a beautifully renovated Neo-Classical mansion, with annexes nearby, including the Ghika Gallery *(see pp26–7)*.

3

7 Kerameikos

Classical Athens' cemetery gives a fascinating cross-section of life, and death, at the city's edge, with elaborate tombs, temples, sacred roads – and an ancient brothel *(see pp30–31)*.

8 Byzantine and Christian Museum

The Byzantine and Christian heritage of modern Greece's territory is told through examples of its works, from the intricacy of precious metalwork to the solemnity of the many icons *(see pp32–3)*.

Philopappos Hill **9**

A green-gladed respite in the city centre, with a wonderful view and a mix of monuments ranging from ancient and Byzantine to modern *(see pp34–5)*.

10 Temple of Olympian Zeus

Ancient Greece's most colossal temple stands beside the monumental arch that divided Athens between Greek hero Theseus and formidable Roman emperor Hadrian *(see pp36–7)*.

🔟⭐ Acropolis

The temples on the "Sacred Rock" of Athens are considered among the most important monuments in the Western world, for they have exerted considerable influence on our monumental architecture since. The great marble masterpieces were constructed during the late 5th-century BC reign of Perikles, the Golden Age of Athens. Most were temples built to honour Athena, the city's patron goddess. Still breathtaking for their proportion and scale, both human and majestic, the temples were adorned with magnificent, dramatic sculptures of the gods.

1 Acropolis Rock

As the highest part of the city, the rock **(main image)** is an ideal place for refuge, religion and royalty. The Acropolis Rock has been used continuously for these purposes since Neolithic times.

6 Erechtheion

Poseidon and Athena are said to have battled for patronage of Athens on this spot. The Erechtheion's design combines temples to each of the two gods **(above)**.

2 Temple of Athena Nike ("Victory")

There has been a temple **(above)** to a goddess of victory at this location since prehistoric times, as it protects and stands over the most vulnerable part of the rock.

3 Propylaia

At the top of the rock, you are greeted by the Propylaia, the grand entrance through which all visitors passed to reach the summit temples.

4 Panathenaic Way

The route used in an ancient procession during which a new tunic, or *peplos*, would have been offered to Athena, along with sacrifices.

5 Parthenon

The epitome of ancient Greek Classical art, a magnificent "Temple to the Virgin", goddess Athena **(left)**. She was represented inside by a giant gold and ivory sculpture.

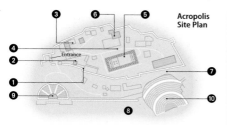

Acropolis Site Plan

Entrance

7 Panagia Chrysospiliotissa

Originally dedicated to the god of wine and revelry, the cave was later turned into the church of the Mother of God of the Golden Cave.

8 Acropolis Museum

The stunning Acropolis Museum *(see pp14–15)* houses around 4,000 artifacts within a space almost 10 times larger than the old museum.

9 Odeon of Herodes Atticus

A late addition to the Acropolis, built in 161 by its namesake. In summer it hosts events of the Athens Festival *(see pp72–3)*.

10 Dionysos Theatre

With a mosaic-tiled stage, this theatre **(below)** held Classical Greece's drama competitions, where tragedies and comedies by great playwrights were performed. It seated 15,000, and you can still see the marble-engraved front-row seats, reserved for priests of Dionysos.

NEED TO KNOW

MAP J5 ■ 210 311 4172
■ www. odysseus.culture.gr

Open Apr–Oct 8am–8pm daily last admission 7:30pm; closes early in winter

Adm €20; students half price. A special €30 ticket allows entry to Kerameikos, Theatre of Dionysos, Agora, Roman Forum, Temple of Olympian Zeus, the Lyckeios and Hadrian's Library (valid for 5 days)

Acropolis Museum: **MAP K5**; Dionysiou Areopagitou 15; 210 900 0900; open Apr–Oct: 8am–8pm Tue–Thu, Sat & Sun (to 4pm Mon & 10pm Fri); Nov–Mar: 9am–5pm Mon–Thu (to 10pm Fri & 8pm Sat & Sun); adm €5; www. theacropolis museum.gr

■ Visit Acropolis first thing in the morning or at sunset to avoid the midday heat and multitudinous tour groups that arrive in droves late morning.

Acropolis Museum

The Caryatids

1 The Caryatids
The original statued pillars that supported the Erechtheion's porch have been brought inside. Their arms are broken now, but initially they held libation bowls.

2 The Parthenon Marbles
The marbles are displayed in the order in which they would have graced the Parthenon, with blank spaces significantly left for sculptures that remain in London.

3 The Calf-Bearer
This joyous Archaic sculpture shows a bearded man carrying a calf, to be offered as a sacrifice to Athena. The statue itself was a votive offering and dates to 570 BC.

4 The Peplos Kore
One of the most exquisite of the Archaic votive statues. Her gown, called a *peplos*, was painted with decorative colours. Traces of paint are still visible on her eyes, lips and curly hair.

5 Kore with Almond-Shaped Eyes
The most sumptuous of the votive *korai* – her detailed drapery and fully formed body show real development in sculpture. Her dress was painted with detailed patterns, including a border with the distinctive "Greek key" pattern.

6 Pediment of the Ancient Temple
Part of the pediment of an ancient temple to Athena, built before the Parthenon and later destroyed, shows Athena fighting against a Titan. It dates to 520 BC.

7 The Kritios Boy
This sculpture of a young male athlete marks the transition from Archaic to early Classical sculpture, with the introduction of a naturalistic pose. The Kritios Boy sculpture dates to 480 BC.

The "Mourning Athena"

8 Relief of the "Mourning Athena"
This tiny relief shows the goddess Athena as a girl, without sword or shield and clad in an Attic *peplos*.

9 The Glass Floor
The museum has been built directly over an early Christian settlement. Glass floors allow visitors to look directly down into the site while approaching the museum entrance from the street.

10 Frieze on the Temple of Athena Nike
The small but dynamically sculpted frieze shows scenes of battle, with gods, Persians and Greeks all stepping into the fray.

MORE THAN A BUILDING

Parthenon marble

The small, worn-around-the-edges museum that clung to one corner of the Acropolis had never really done justice to the stunning treasures it held within. But the modern, all-glass showpiece of a museum at the foot of the Acropolis does. The old museum closed in July 2007 in anticipation of the move to the Acropolis Museum, which opened mid-2008. However, there was an ulterior motive to the construction of this museum, which was to send a pointed international message. Between 1800 and 1803, the seventh Earl of Elgin removed two-thirds of the sculptures of gods, men and monsters adorning the Parthenon and took them to England. Most were sold to the British Museum, which refuses to return them, saying that the sculptures are integral to its role in narrating human cultural achievement. The Acropolis Museum has answered previous criticism that Athens could not display them adequately or safely, for a special room awaits the return. Greece hopes that when thousands of international visitors see the sparkling but empty showcase, it will increase the pressure on Britain, forcing a much-anticipated return of the marbles.

TOP 10
SCENES DEPICTED IN THE PARTHENON MARBLES

1 The birth of Athena, springing fully formed out of Zeus's head *(see p52)*

2 The Pantheon watching Athena's birth

3 Athena and Poseidon's fight for control of the city *(see p52)*

4 The gods watch and take sides in Athena and Poseidon's battle

5 The Panathenaic Procession, ancient Athens' most important religious event

6 The battle of the Centaurs and Lapiths

7 The battle of the gods and the Titans

8 The battle of the Greeks and the Amazons

9 The sack of Troy

10 Priestesses prepare a veil for Athena

At the Acropolis Museum, glass walls allow a direct view of the Acropolis temples from within the museum, while the glass floor offers a view over the ruins of an early Christian settlement.

⭐ The Agora

Athens' ancient marketplace, founded in the 6th century BC, was the heart of the city for 1,200 years. It was the centre for all civic activities, including politics, commerce, philosophy, religion, arts and athletics. This is where Socrates addressed his public, where democracy was born and where St Paul preached. Because of its varied uses, the rambling site can be confusing. Compared to the sweltering Acropolis, the grassy Agora is a relaxing place to wander, as you imagine the lively bustle that once filled this historic centre.

① Temple of Hephaistos

The best-preserved Classical temple in Greece **(above)**, devoted jointly to Hephaistos and Athena. Its fantastical frieze depicts the deeds of Theseus and Herakles.

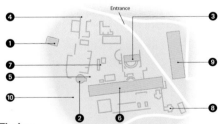

Agora Site Plan

② Tholos

The executive committee of the first parliament lived and worked in this circular building, also known as the Prytaneion.

③ Odeon of Agrippa

Marcus Vipsanius Agrippa, an official with the first emperor Augustus, had this theatre built in AD 15. Outside stood statues of three serpent-tailed Giants and Tritons on huge plinths **(left)**. Two Tritons and a Giant remain.

④ Stoa Basileios

Built in 500 BC, this building housed the office of legal affairs concerning ancient cults. Most of it was destroyed when the Heruli invaded and sacked Athens in AD 267. Its ruins are best viewed from Adrianou.

5 Monument of the Eponymous Heroes

Citizens were divided into 10 tribes (*phylae*), each represented by a different Attican hero. Dated 350 BC, this monument had bronze statues of each representative tribal hero: Antiochos, Ajax, Kekrops, Hippothoon, Erechtheus, Aigeas, Leos, Akamas, Pandion and Oeneus.

6 Middle Stoa

The large Middle Stoa **(above)** took up the major part of the central marketplace, its aisles lined with Doric columns.

7 Altar of Zeus Agoraios

This lavish temple to the ruler of the gods was originally built elsewhere in Athens (possibly the Pnyx) in the 4th century BC. In the first century AD, it was dismantled, brought to the Agora and reconstructed.

8 Nymphaion

The ruins of the Nymphaion, an elaborate 2nd-century fountain-house, are still visible, despite the building of Agii Apostoli church over it in the 11th century.

SITE OF PILGRIMAGE

You may well see people on the Areopagos, the rock above the Agora, praying or singing hymns. Pilgrims from around the world retracing the steps of Paul converge here, the site named in the Bible (Acts 17:22–34) where the saint gave his famous "Sermon to an Unknown God" speech. This spoke of the errors of ancient Greek religions, and here Paul converted the first Athenians to Christianity, including Dionysios the Areopagite.

10 Great Drain

When Athens experiences a downpour, the Great Drain **(above)** still collects runoff from the Acropolis and Agora, and sends it to the now usually dry Eridanos river.

NEED TO KNOW

MAP B4 ■ Adrianou 24, Monastiraki ■ 210 32 10 185 ■ www. odysseus culture.gr

Open 8am–8pm daily; last adm 7:45pm (closes early in winter, call ahead to confirm)

Adm €8, or included in €30 Acropolis ticket

■ The best overview of the Agora is from the Areopagos rock *(see p61)*.

■ Head to the local favourite Dioskouri, situated at Dioskouron 13, overlooking the Agora. It serves coffee and snacks, with outdoor tables lined along scenic steps.

9 Stoa of Attalos

King Attalos II of Pergamon (159–138 BC) built this impressive two-storey structure **(above)**. It was reconstructed in 1956 by the American School of Archaeology. Today the Stoa is a world-class museum displaying finds from the Agora *(see pp18–19)*.

Agora Museum (Stoa of Attalos)

1 Head of Nike

This small, delicate head of Athena Nike, dated to about 425 BC, was once covered with sheets of silver and gold; eyes would have been inset.

2 Klepsydra

Dating back to the 5th century BC, this is a unique example of the terracotta water clocks used for timing speeches in the public law courts. When a speaker began, the stopper was pulled out of the jug. It would take exactly six minutes for the water to run out, at which point the speaker had to stop, even if he was in mid-sentence.

3 Ostraka

These small inscribed pottery fragments played a crucial role in the incipient democracy. Called *ostraka*, they were used as ballots in the process of ostracism. When there was fear of a tyranny, citizens voted to exile politicians considered dangerous to democracy. Those displayed show the names of several prominent politicians exiled in this way, including Themistokles, one of Athens' most important leaders.

Ostraka fragments

4 Bronze Shield

This huge Spartan shield was a trophy taken by the Athenians after their victory over the Spartans in the battle of Sphacteria, in 425 BC. It is a vast object, and it is difficult to imagine a soldier carrying something so heavy and cumbersome into the melee of battle. On the front of the shield, one of the Athenian victors has inscribed, "Athens defeated Sparta at Pylos".

5 Aryballos

This small Archaic oil-flask sculpted in the form of a kneeling boy represents an athlete binding a ribbon, a symbol of victory, around his head. It dates to around 530 BC.

Aryballos

6 Winged Nike

This sensuous, swirling, rippling statue of Athena once adorned the Agora's Stoa of Zeus Eleutherios. Her active stance and clinging, flowing *chiton* (a loose, full-length tunic) are typical of the way in which the goddess was depicted at that time. It dates to around 415 BC.

7 Apollo Patroös

This colossal but finely sculpted marble cult statue of Apollo graced a temple to the god in the Agora. A later copy shows that in this sculpture the god of music was playing the kithara, an early stringed instrument. Dating to around 335 BC, it is the work of the famous Greek sculptor and painter Euphranor.

Apollo Patroös

8 Athenian Law for Democracy

In 337 or 336 BC, the citizens of Athena passed a historic vote for a new system of democracy, giving every (male) citizen an equal vote. The law is inscribed here, and topped by an image of a personification of the Demos (people) of Athens being crowned by Democracy herself.

⑨ Marble Kleroterion

This device was used by the Parliament of Athens between the 3rd and 2nd century BC, in the period of the ten tribes of Attica, to select people randomly for official roles. The seemingly simple box performed operations with slots, weights, cranks and coloured balls. A sign below the display case explains the complexities of its operation.

⑩ Calyx Krater

Dating to 530 BC, this is the earliest known calyx krater – an elegant vessel used to mix water and wine at banquets – and the only vase of this shape attributed to Exekias, the greatest Attic vase painter. It shows several beautifully detailed scenes, including Herakles being introduced to the gods of Olympos and the Greek and Trojan heroes' fight over the body of Patroklos.

THE STOA OF ATTALOS

The Stoa of Attalos was originally a 2nd-century BC shopping mall. Both arcades were divided into shops, and the cool marble-pillared space was a popular place for wealthy Athenians to meet and gossip. Through decades of excavations, the Agora has become recognized as one of Greece's most important sites, yielding finds precious for their artistic quality and ability to tell important stories about political and cultural life in the first democracy. During the 1950s, the American School of Archaeology reconstructed the Stoa and converted the building into a museum to display finds from the site. Most of the museum's exhibits are closely connected with the development of democracy in Athens. Outside, in the marble passage, statues that once adorned the temples in the marketplace are displayed.

Head of Nike

The reconstructed Stoa of Attalos, home of the Agora Museum

TOP 10 ★ National Archaeological Museum

More than just the best museum in Greece, this is one of the most important and exciting museums in the world. It is packed with famous, influential and beautiful works, from the Neolithic Age, to the great Bronze Age cultures described by Homer, to the Golden Age of Classical Athens, up to the Roman era. Highlights include numerous gold artefacts found at Mycenae and elegant Archaic *kouroi* and *korai* statues.

Thera Frescoes ②
The highly advanced settlement of Akrotiri, on the ancient island of Thera (now Santorini), was buried after a volcanic eruption in the 17th century BC. Beautiful frescoes, such as these boxer boys **(right)**, were perfectly preserved under the ash.

③ Archaic Kouroi/Korai, 7th Century BC–480 BC
Used in temples and graves, these statues of idealised youths and maidens were the first monumental works in Greek art. The earliest are stiff and stylized, but through the 6th century, artists learnt to depict the body more naturally.

① Cycladic Collection, 3200–2200 BC
The Cycladic Museum *(see pp22–3)* has the largest collection from this civilization, but here you'll find some of the most unusual pieces, such as this harp-player **(above)**, showing, unusually, a three-dimensional figure in action.

Mycenaean Collection, 16th– 11th Centuries BC ④
The Mycenaeans were famed both for their prowess as warriors and for the gold amassed by their traders. Parts of those hoards are displayed here, including the "Agamemnon" death mask **(right)** and priceless golden swords and jewellery.

⑤ Bronze Collection
This, the richest collection of bronze works from the Archaic and Classical eras, includes a majestic 460 BC sculpture of Poseidon or Zeus **(left)**, a 140 BC sculpture of a galloping horse and a youth of Antikythira.

6 Classical Statuary

The collection includes original marble sculptures from temples all around Greece. Highlights are those that adorned the Temple of Asklepios at Epidauros, works such as the 100 BC Diadoumenos and a marble copy of a late-5th-century bronze by the great sculptor Polykleitos.

7 Hellenistic Statuary

Here the stiff monuments of the Archaic period give way to sculptures that are full of vigorous movement and sensuality. This is especially so in the 100 BC group of Aphrodite, Pan and Eros, and the statue of a wounded Gaul.

8 Vases and Minor Art Collection

The collection contains impressive vases, terracotta figurines, gold jewels and glass vessels, dated from the 10th century BC up to the 18th century AD.

9 Egyptian Wing

This collection, from the Neolithic period to the end of the Roman era, is fascinating to view in conjunction with the earliest Greek Archaic art, which borrowed from Egyptian statuary before developing its very own style. The collection includes a funerary boat sculpted from wood **(below)**.

EARTHQUAKE

In September 1999, the strongest earthquake in a century rocked Athens, sending buildings tumbling and, in the National Archaeological Museum, shattering fragile pots. About half the museum was subsequently closed to the public, but reopened after a gradual refurbishment between 2002 to 2005.

10 Grave Stelae

Classical marble grave sculptures **(below)** became so opulent by the end of the 4th century BC that they were banned. The scenes in these beautiful carvings typically show the deceased on the right, the bereaved on the left.

NEED TO KNOW

MAP C1 ▪ 44 Patision (28 Oktovriou) ▪ 213 21 44 800 ▪ www.namuseum.gr

Open Apr–Oct: 8am–8pm Tue–Sun (from 1pm Mon); closes early Nov–Mar

Adm €10 (free first Sun of the month, Nov–Mar)

▪ There's much to see here that it makes sense to go twice. Buy the short informational guide books available at the museum.

▪ There is an atrium café inside, and a larger café in the plaza out front.

TOP 10 ⭐ Museum of Cycladic Art

A delightful setting in which to ponder elegant, semi-abstract Cycladic figurines – remnants of a culture that flourished in the Cyclades from 3200–2000 BC. The beautiful marble carvings are unlike anything found in contemporary civilizations. Most are female forms – perhaps symbolic companions for the deceased – and their elemental shapes have inspired many 20th-century artists.

Red-Figure Column Krater ②

This vase **(right)**, attributed to the Agrigento Painter, active in Attica in the 5th century BC, shows a girl musician playing a double flute and a young man holding a lyre. Between them is a dancing youth. The group is led by an ivy-wreathed boy carrying an amphora on his shoulders.

① Dove Vase

Carved entirely from one block of marble, this vase, decorated with doves **(above)**, is the most remarkable of a series of vessels found in tombs. Archaeologists believe birds held an important meaning for the Cycladic culture, since they appear in many other carvings as well – but the nature of that significance remains to be established.

③ "Modigliani" Figure

So-called because the lines of this figure **(left)** show up clearly in the work of painter Amedeo Modigliani (1884–1920). The slender, simple shape, crossed arms and smooth face are all classic Cycladic traits. Figures with feet that are incapable of support indicate that they would probably have been lying down.

④ Female Figurine

The limestone female figurine has deep eye sockets and modelled breasts. It belongs to a group of human-form sculptures from the Chalcolithic period (3500–2800 BC in the Cyclades).

Bronze Helmets ⑤

The Corinthian helmet underwent quite a development in the 7th century BC, with the shape being progressively altered in order to fit better on the head. It was the first helmet to be fashioned from a single bronze sheet, and it protected every part of the head **(right)**.

6 Symposium Kylix

This exceptional piece of 5th-century BC pottery **(below)** shows a naked youth drawing wine from a large mixing vessel, known as a krater, to fill the cup he holds in his left hand. According to the inscription, the young man is named Lysis, and his beauty is praised by the addition of the epithet "fair".

Plan of the Museum of Cycladic Art

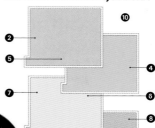

Key to Floorplan
- Cycladic Art
- Ancient Greek Art
- Ancient Cypriot Art
- Scenes from Daily Life in Antiquity

7 Dionysos Vase

This beautifully preserved 6th-century BC vase shows the god of wine and revelry Dionysos on one side (flanked by dancing satyrs) and, on the other side, Athena and Hermes conversing.

8 Male Figure

The only male figure of its size found so far in the prototypical Cycladic style. Attributed by some scholars to the Goulandris Master, who created the finest female figures, it has the same shape and placement of the arms. The separated legs indicate a standing pose, rather than the typically prone pose of the female figures.

9 Hunter-Warrior and Queen

The male and female figures, with elongated arms and almond-shaped eyes, are the most naturalistic of the later Cycladic figures. Experts believe that the dagger carved around the male figure indicates that he was a hunter-warrior.

NEED TO KNOW

MAP P3 ■ Neofytou Douka 4 and Vasilissis Sofias ■ 210 72 28 321 ■ www.cycladic.gr

Open 10am–5pm Mon, Wed–Sun (to 8pm Thu, from 11am Sun); closed Tue

Adm €7 (€3.50 for permanent exhibits); adm higher for special exhibits (except on Mon)

■ All the featured exhibits are found in the main building of the Cycladic Wing, while the Stathatos Mansion shows temporary exhibitions.

■ It's best to visit until after 1pm as mornings are crowded with tour groups.

■ The museum's atrium café makes a great spot for a light lunch.

10 Stathatos Mansion

In 1991, the museum took over the adjoining Stathatos Mansion, a gilded Neo-Classical confection by Bavarian architect Ernst Ziller *(see p102)*. Here the museum hosts all temporary exhibitions, receptions and lectures **(above)**.

TOP 10 ★ Roman Forum and Tower of the Winds

During the first century AD, the Romans moved Athens' marketplace here from the old Agora. Smaller than the original, the marble-pillared courtyard was a grander place to set up shop, and this became the city's commercial and administrative centre until the 19th century. Its greatest attraction was the unique and brilliantly designed Tower of the Winds.

3 Tower of the Winds

The octagonal tower **(left)**, built by Syrian astronomer Andronikos Kyrrhestas in 50 BC, has personifications of the eight winds on each side. Inside, a water clock was operated by a stream from the Acropolis.

4 Fethiye Mosque

During the Ottoman occupation, the Forum remained important. This "Mosque of the Conquest" was built soon after Sultan Mehmet II took Athens in June 1456. After its long restoration, the interior has been opened for visitors.

1 Byzantine Grave Markers

In Byzantine times, when the Tower of the Winds was used as a church, the area around it was a cemetery. Graves were marked with cylindrical engraved markers, some of which were quite beautiful. These were later gathered in one place, along with others from around Athens.

2 Vespasianae (68-seat Public Latrine)

The pleasantly situated marble facility was housed in a rectangular building with a court-yard in the middle, and latrines lining all four sides. Proximity wasn't a problem – latrines were social gathering places.

5 Courtyard

This was the centre of activity. The courtyard was surrounded by shops and workshops selling food, cloth, ceramics, jewellery and wares from abroad. The Emperor Hadrian had the courtyard paved in the 2nd century AD.

6 Fountain

This splashing marble fountain **(below)**, whose waters, like those of the water clock, may also have been sourced from the Acropolis, once provided cool relief to market-goers. But stay away from the brackish water that occasionally fills it today.

7 Gate of Athena Archegetis

The four-columned western entrance to the forum **(left)** is built of Pentelic marble. It was dedicated by the people of Athens to the goddess Athena in her avatar of Archegetis, "(S)he Who Commands".

A MISCELLANY OF FINDS

Ever since the 1940s, archaeologists have used the forum as a repository for small, unclassifiable finds from all over Attica. Thus the site is studded with out-of-place but fascinating extras, such as the wall of mismatched capital pieces near the Vespasianae, and the garlanded sarcophagus, about which little is known, by the fountain.

Roman columns and the Fethiye Mosque behind

8 East Propylon

This is one of the two original entrances to the marketplace. In a stoa next to it are sculptures of important Romans, probably officials or emperors, which marketgoers would have seen while coming and going.

9 Agoranomeion

This two-roomed building was long believed to be the office of market officials. Latest theories reckon it was a part of a cult to Athena Archegetis or all Roman emperors.

NEED TO KNOW

MAP J4–K4 ■ Monastiraki ■ 210 324 5220 ■ www.odysseus.culture.gr

Open 8am–3pm daily (until 5pm Sat & Sun)

Adm €6 (students half price), or included in €30 Acropolis ticket

■ During the full moon in August there may still be a free moonlit classical concert here. There is free admission until 1am on the night of the August full moon.

■ Most restaurants around the Roman Forum are crowded and over-priced. Head to Thanassis just off Monastiraki Square *(see p83)* for a great lunch of Egyptian-style kebabs.

Map of the Roman Forum

10 Inscription on Gate of Athena Archegetis

A faint inscription on the *architrave* (the horizontal architectural structure at the top) comemmorates the contruction of this gate between 11 to 9 BC by the citizens of Athens, during the term of the archon Nikias.

⭐ Benaki Museum

This vast museum gives a panoramic view of Greek history from the Stone Age (7000 BC) to the 20th century, by way of Classical Greece and the eras of the Byzantine and Ottoman empires. Over 20,000 objects are laid out in chronological order in 36 rooms, showing the evolution of Greek painting, sculpture and handicrafts.

1 Paintings by El Greco

Domenikos Theotokopoulos (1541–1614) became known as El Greco in Spain. Two early works here, completed while the artist was still in his native Crete, include *St Luke Painting the Panagia Odigitria* (left), painted between 1560 and 1567.

2 Thebes Treasure

During the late Bronze Age, ornamental jewellery was used to display personal wealth. This hoard of Mycenaean gold jewellery includes an engraved gold signet ring, depicting a sacred marriage connected to the worship of a prehistoric goddess.

3 Thessaly Treasure

This stunning display of Hellenistic gold jewellery from the 3rd–2nd centuries BC employs filigree and granulation (beads of gold soldered onto metal) to produce minutely crafted earrings, necklaces, bracelets and diadems. One of the highlights is a decorative band with a knot of Herakles at its centre.

4 The Building

This Neo-Classical mansion of 1867 (above) was bought by Emmanuel Benakis in 1910, passed to his children, and then presented to the state in 1931 when it opened as a museum.

5 Mid-18th-Century Reception Room

The richly painted and gilded wooden ceiling and panelled walls of this room (below) – a reconstruction from a Macedonian mansion – recall a time when these crafts flourished locally.

6 Café

Cultural overload? Take a break on the rooftop terrace café overlooking the trees and lawns of the National Gardens.

NEED TO KNOW

MAP N3 ■ Koumbari 1, Kolonaki ■ 210 367 1000 ■ www.benaki.gr

Open 10am–6pm Wed & Fri, 10am–midnight Thu & Sat, 10am–4pm Sun ■ Closed Mon & Tue

Adm permanent exhibits: €9; temporary exhibits: €7; under 22s free

■ Bear in mind that the museum has free admission and late-night opening every Thursday.

■ It is almost impossible to see the entire Benaki collection in one go: explore one section in the morning, stop for lunch in the rooftop café, then see the rest in the afternoon.

⑦ Evvia Treasure

Around 3000 BC, the introduction of metallurgy marked the transition from the Stone Age to the Bronze Age. Outstanding examples from this period are three cups, two gold **(below)** and one silver, hammered into simple forms with minimal decoration. They date from between 3000 and 2800 BC.

⑧ A Second Room from Kozani

Another reconstruction from Macedonia, this mid-19th-century reception room features a minutely carved wooden ceiling, ornate built-in wooden cupboards and a low seating area, complete with Persian rugs and cushions, and a wrought-iron coffee table.

WHO WAS BENAKIS?

Antonis Benakis (1873–1954) was born in Egypt to an immensely wealthy merchant, Emmanuel Benakis, who later became Mayor of Athens. Antonis began collecting Islamic art while in Alexandria and went on to collect Byzantine art and Greek folk art once in Athens. He donated the entire collection to the Greek state in 1931. His sister, Penelope Delta (1874–1941), was a much-loved author of children's books.

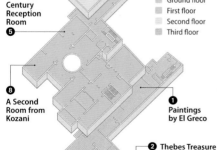

Floorplan of the Benaki Museum

Café ⑥

Mid-18th-Century Reception Room ⑤

⑧ A Second Room from Kozani

Thessaly Treasure ③

The Building ④

Entrance

⑨ Greek Independence Memorabilia

Key to Floorplan
- ▓ Ground floor
- ▓ First floor
- ▓ Second floor
- ▓ Third floor

① Paintings by El Greco

② Thebes Treasure

⑦ Evvia Treasure

⑩ Shop

⑨ Greek Independence Memorabilia

Finely decorated swords, sabres and rifles, a painting of a freedom fighter from 1821, the flag of Hydra island **(below)** proclaiming "either victory or death", and a writing desk belonging to Lord Bryon are among the displays.

⑩ Shop

Here, exhibits such as ceramic bowls and tiles, jewellery and Byzantine icons have been carefully produced, using original craft techniques where possible.

Following pages View over Plaka from Acropolis towards Lykavittos Hill

★ Kerameikos

Ancient Athens' outer walls run through Kerameikos, once the edge of the Classical city. Warriors and priestesses returned to Athens via two separate roads through here (one leading to a brothel, the other to a temple). Statesmen and heroes were buried beneath showy tombs lining the roads. But Kerameikos was also the scene of far shadier activities: the haunt of prostitutes, money-lenders and wine-sellers.

Pompeiion ①
The Pompeiion **(right)** was used to prepare for festive and religious processions, especially the annual Panathenaic procession, in which a new garment was brought to the statue of Athena in the Parthenon.

② **City Walls**
The walls, which surrounded the entire city, were built by Athenian ruler Themistokles between 487 and 479 BC. They incorporated materials from all over the city, including marble from tombs, temples and houses.

④ **Dipylon**
The main roads from Thebes, Corinth and the Peloponnese converged at this entrance gate to Athens, the largest in ancient Greece. Many ceremonial events were held here to mark arrivals and departures.

⑥ **Sanctuary of the Tritopatores**
It is uncertain who exactly the Tritopatores were, but they may have been representatives of the souls of the dead, and worshipped in an ancestor cult.

⑤ **Marble Bull**
The bull of the tomb of Dionysios of Kollytos from 4th century BC **(below)** is the most recognizable monument here. Its inscriptions show Dionysios was praised for his goodness, and died unmarried, mourned by his mother and sisters.

③ **Sacred Gate**
Through this well-preserved gate **(above)** passed the Sacred Way, reserved for pilgrims and priestesses during the procession to Eleusis *(see p115)*. A great marble sphinx was built into the gate.

Plan of Kerameikos

NEED TO KNOW

MAP A3–4

■ Ermou 148, Thisio

■ 210 34 63 552

Open Apr–Oct: 8am–8pm daily; last admission 7:45pm; earlier closure in winter.

Adm: €8, or included with €30 Acropolis ticket; entry to site museum included

■ The green site and surrounding industrial buildings are at their most eerily lovely in the early evening, when they are tinged pink by the setting sun.

■ There are several reasonably priced tavernas lining the nearby streets of Apostolou Pavlou and Eptahalkou. Head to either for a traditional outdoor lunch.

THE OLD POTTERS' DISTRICT

The name Kerameikos comes from Keramos, the patron god of ceramics. According to Pausanias (see p51) and other early writers, the name recalls an age-old group of potters' workshops that used to be located on the grassy banks of the river Eridanos, which cuts through the site. The museum contains fine examples of Greek urns and other pottery found at the site.

⑧ Warriors' Tombs

The high, round burial mounds (tumuli) lining the sacred way date from the 7th century BC and were probably first built to honour great warriors. Most have marble coffins and offerings at their centres, with the mounds built up around them.

⑨ Stele of Hegeso

This lovely grave pediment is one of the finest works of 5th-century BC Attic art. Hegeso, the dead woman, is portrayed seated, taking a trinket from a box. The original is in the National Archaeological Museum.

⑦ Kerameikos Museum

This site (above) is packed with fascinating finds, such as originals of many tombs replaced by casts and pottery shards of erotic scenes from a brothel.

⑩ Tomb of Dexileos

This marble-relief carved tomb (below) is of a young horseman who died in 394 BC. Unlike here, the dead of ancient Greece were often depicted along with their living family, saying a final goodbye.

TOP 10 ⭐ Byzantine and Christian Museum

From c. AD 330 to 1204, the Byzantine Empire prevailed in the Mediterranean region. The wealthy Orthodox Church was the most important influence in Byzantium, and left behind a vast legacy. This collection embraces 15,000 objects taken from that period.

1 Shepherd Carrying a Lamb
This 4th-century marble sculpture is also a Christian allegory with pagan roots. Though the shepherd is meant to be Christ, the image is taken directly from an Archaic sculpture found on the Acropolis of a man bringing a calf to be sacrificed to the goddess Athena.

2 Treasury of Mytilene
A collection of 6th-century silver vessels, gold jewellery and coins, discovered in a sunken ship off the island of Mytilene (Lesvos). Scholars believe the valuables were brought to the island to be hidden, and were never recovered by their owners.

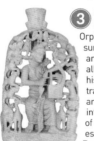

3 Orpheus Playing a Lyre
Orpheus (**left**) is surrounded by animals, creating an allegory of Christ and his followers. This transmutation of ancient pagan myths into the new religion of Christianity was an essential element of Byzantine art.

5 Mosaic Icon of the Mother of God (The Episkepsis)
This 13th-century mosaic (**above**) shows the Mother of God and Child, in the pose known as *Glykophiloussa*, imploring Her Son to save the world. Mosaic icons are rare – only about 40 are known to exist – and all originate from Constantinople.

4 Precious Ecclesiastical Artifacts
This case contains a late 14th-century wooden cross covered with silver and embellished with small steatite icons, a 10th-century copper chalice, and a 14th-century silk stole decorated with holy figures embroidered in metallic and silk thread.

NEED TO KNOW

MAP P3 ▪ Vasilissis Sofias 22 ▪ 213 213 9517 ▪ www.byzantine museum.gr

Open 8am–8pm Tue–Sun (from noon Mon); closes at 4pm during winter; site is cleared 20 mins before closing

Adm €8; students €4; under 18s free

▪ In summer, there are often concerts in the court-yard. Call ahead to find out what's on and when.

▪ There is a café-bistro located in the museum garden. Alternatively, head to one of the tavernas in nearby, lively Pangráti district or in Kolonaki.

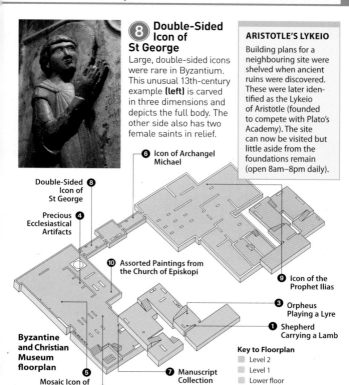

8 Double-Sided Icon of St George

Large, double-sided icons were rare in Byzantium. This unusual 13th-century example (left) is carved in three dimensions and depicts the full body. The other side also has two female saints in relief.

ARISTOTLE'S LYKEIO

Building plans for a neighbouring site were shelved when ancient ruins were discovered. These were later identified as the Lykeio of Aristotle (founded to compete with Plato's Academy). The site can now be visited but little aside from the foundations remain (open 8am–8pm daily).

6 Icon of Archangel Michael

Double-Sided 8 Icon of St George

Precious 4 Ecclesiastical Artifacts

10 Assorted Paintings from the Church of Episkopi

9 Icon of the Prophet Ilias

3 Orpheus Playing a Lyre

1 Shepherd Carrying a Lamb

Byzantine and Christian Museum floorplan

Key to Floorplan
- Level 2
- Level 1
- Lower floor

5 Mosaic Icon of the Mother of God (The Episkepsis)

2 Treasury of Mytilene

7 Manuscript Collection

6 Icon of Archangel Michael

Set in a glowing field of gold, this 14th-century icon from Constantinople depicts the Archangel Michael with a sceptre and orb, symbolic of the terrestrial world.

7 Manuscript Collection

The highlight of this collection is an early 14th-century imperial *chrysobull* (edict) issued by Emperor Andronikos II Paleologos. The top of the scroll bears a miniature showing the emperor himself handing a document to Christ, while at the bottom, the emperor's signature appears in red ink.

9 Icon of the Prophet Ilias

This late 17th-century icon, titled *The Ascension of the Prophet Ilias and Scenes from his Life,* is signed by Cretan artist Theodore Poulakis. It depicts the prophet riding a flaming chariot. Elijah (Ilias in Greek), along with Jesus and the Panagia, is the only biblical character to physically ascend to heaven.

10 Assorted Paintings from the Church of Episkopi

Probably created during the 17th century, the *temblon* (icon screen) paintings (below) depict biblical scenes. Other paintings dating back to the 9th, 11th and 13th centuries are displayed as they would have been in the old Evrytanian church.

TOP 10 ★ Philopappos Hill

The pine-covered slopes of Philopappos Hill offer a pleasantly shaded maze of paths leading through monuments marking centuries of history. Known as "the hill of muses" in antiquity, it has been a source of inspiration for countless poets. On the first Monday of Lent, the hill swarms with hundreds of Athenians, who gather here to fly kites.

4 Socrates' Prison

This is believed to be the cave **(left)** where Socrates *(see p50)* was imprisoned, having been condemned to death. His disciples sat with him as he drank the hemlock that dispatched him.

1 The Deme of Koile

This ancient road leads from the Acropolis to Piraeus, passing between Philopappos Hill and the Pnyx to follow the course of the Long Walls (5th century BC). It was a two-lane road, 8–12 m (26–40 ft) wide, with anti-slip grooves. A 500-m (1,600-ft) stretch has been excavated.

5 The Pnyka

If Athens is the cradle of democracy, this spot **(right)** is its exact birthplace. After Athens became a demo-cracy in 508 BC, the first ever democratic congress met here weekly, and the greatest orators held forth. The limestone theatre, cut into the hill, accommo-dated over 10,000.

2 Old National Observatory

Greece's oldest research centre is housed in a beautiful Neo-Classical building. The centre monitors astronomy, weather and, especially, the earthquakes that occasionally rattle Athens.

3 Hill of the Nymphs

In ancient times, Greeks believed Philopappos was inhabited by the muses of art, music and poetry. This smaller hill was home to the nymphs – the female spirits of trees, mountain tops and springs.

6 Church of Agia Marina

Agia Marina **(below)** is associated with childbirth and sick children, and pregnant women used to come here and slip down a carved slide to ensure a safe delivery. In the past, mothers brought sick children here to spend the night. A colourful festival honours Marina on 16th and 17th July every year.

7 Church of Agios Dimitrios Lombardiaris

In 1648, an Ottoman commander planned to bombard this charming Byzantine church. But lightning struck his cannon, giving the church the epithet 'Lombardiaris', a corruption of Bombardier.

8 Philopappos Monument

Syrian-born prince and Roman consul, Gaius Julius Antiochus Philopappos, admired Classical Greek culture. He retired in Athens and died here in about AD 114. The Greeks built a marble tomb and monument **(left)** after two years showing him as an Athenian citizen, surrounded by his royal Commagene family. Its partially destroyed form looks across to the Acropolis.

THE 1687 SIEGE

During an attempt to seize the Ottoman-occupied Acropolis, the Venetians garrisoned themselves on Philopappos Hill, the perfect strategic location to shell their target. Too perfect, unfortunately – one of their shells hit the Parthenon, where the Turks stored their gunpowder, and the ensuing explosion severely damaged the Acropolis's prized temple and sculptures.

9 Hilltop View

You may not feel that you deserve such a jaw-dropping view after such an easy, shaded walk. But the hilltop directly overlooks the Acropolis and all of southern Athens stretching to the sea. This was once a favourite vantage-point for generals – and it's equally appealing to photographers today.

NEED TO KNOW

MAP B6 ■ Enter from Dionysiou Areopagitou

Dora Stratou Dance Theatre:
MAP C5 ■ Performances late May–late Sep: 9:30pm Wed–Fri, 8:30pm Sat & Sun, call to confirm. Tickets from the theatre, or call 2103 244 395

■ Though perfectly safe during the day, the unlit paths of Philopappos Hill are best avoided after dark.

■ There is a café, Loumbardiaris, among the trees just behind the frescoed Church of Agios Dimitrios Lombardiaris. Stop here for refreshments and food before walking up to the top of the hill. On the west lies Petralona district, full of good-value tavernas.

10 Dora Stratou Dance Theatre

In 1953, Dora Stratou founded a dance troupe which toured Greece, learning hundreds of endangered regional dances that preserve Greek culture. The troupe still presents the intricate steps.

Map of Philoppapos Hill

Temple of Olympian Zeus

The majestic temple to the ruler of the pantheon was the largest on mainland Greece. Inside stood two colossal statues: one of the god in gold and ivory, and one of the Roman Emperor Hadrian. Though the temple's construction began in 515 BC, political turmoil delayed its completion for nearly 700 years. To thank Hadrian for finishing it, in AD 131 the Athenians built a two-storey arch next to the temple, whose inscription announces Hadrian's claim on the city.

1 Valerian Wall
Enclosing several buildings within the temple complex was a wall **(below)** commissioned by the Roman emperor Valerian in the 3rd century AD. Many of the temples it surrounded were demolished to provide marble for the wall.

WHY DID IT TAKE SO LONG TO BUILD?

The tyrant Peisistratos started the Temple of Olympian Zeus in 515 BC to keep the rebellious Athenians occupied. After his fall in 510 BC, the work ceased. In 175 BC, Syrian king Antiochos IV of Epiphanes resumed the construction work, but it stopped with his death in 164 BC. Finally, Emperor Hadrian (ruled AD 117–138) overlooked the completion of the temple and also personally consecrated it in AD 131–132

2 Temple of Olympian Zeus
Zeus had long been worshipped on this site, and there was at least one other temple to him before this one. Sixteen magnificent columns **(above)** survive from the original 104.

Hadrian's Arch 3
Emperor Hadrian had the west side of this arch **(right)** inscribed "This is Athens, the ancient city of Theseus", and the east side "This is the city of Hadrian and not of Theseus", distinguishing the cities of ancient legend and Roman reality.

4 Themistoklean Gates

Around the site are remains of the wall built by political leader Themistokles in 479 BC, to defend Athens from continuing onslaughts by the Persians.

5 Law Court at the Delphinion

Now mostly in ruins, this law court, from 500 BC, is thought to be on the site of the palace of mythical king Aegeas, the father of Theseus (see p53).

9 Roman Baths

Among the many ruins of "Hadrianopolis", the first structures of Hadrian's new city, are these foundations (above), actually the best-preserved Roman bath house in Athens. It once had a coloured mosaic floor.

10 Temple of Apollo Delphinios and Artemis Delphinia

The temple was built to honour the god-and-goddess siblings Apollo and Artemis, celebrating them in the form of two dolphins.

6 Ruins of Houses

Ancient pipes, foundations and domestic objects show that people lived and built houses here between the 5th century BC and 2nd century AD – the whole time it took to build the temple.

7 Temple of Kronos and Rhea

This temple to Zeus's parents was built in the 5th century BC; now only the foundations remain. Rhea saved Zeus from Kronos, then Zeus took dominion of the universe as ruler of the gods.

8 Temple of Zeus Panhellenios

Hadrian promoted the cult of Zeus Panhellenios ("ruler of all the Greeks") and associated himself with the god. Offers to god and emperor were made in this temple, later demolished for the Valerian wall.

NEED TO KNOW

MAP L5 ■ Leoforos Vas. Olgas 1 at Amalias ■ 210 92 26 330 ■ odysseus.culture.gr

Open 8am–8pm daily. Last admission 7:45pm; earlier closure in winter.

Adm €6, or included with €30 Acropolis ticket

■ To get the best light for photographs of the column capitals, come between 3 and 4pm.

■ For a delicious bite head across Vassilisis Olgas to Aegli Café-Bistro, or across Leoforos Syngrou to one of the many tavernas around Platia Tsokri or Akropoli metro station.

Map of the Temple Site

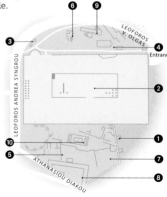

The Top 10
of Everything

Archaeological display at the
Acropolis Museum, Athens

🔟 Moments in History

1 Birth of Athens
The Acropolis was first inhabited in Neolithic times (around 3000 BC), and began to take on the form of a city when it was fortified by the Mycenaeans (inhabitants of the southeastern Greek mainland) in about 1400 BC.

2 Golden Age
The city-state developed into a colonial power in the 6th and 5th centuries BC. Under Perikles (495–429 BC) Athens enjoyed its greatest period of building, when the Parthenon, Erechtheion and Temple of Nike were erected. Cultural life flourished until Sparta's defeat of Athens in the Peloponnesian War (431–404 BC).

Bust of the Greek statesman Perikles

3 Roman Athens
Roman rule began in 146 BC and lasted five centuries. Athenians initially maintained good relations with their rulers, but in 86 BC Athens sided with rebel King Mithridates of Pontos and was sacked by Sulla. Emperor Hadrian (AD 76–138) remained a great admirer of Greek culture, however, and finished the Greek Zeus sanctuary. Later, in about AD 150, Herode Atticus funded the great theatre *(see p13)* that bears his name.

4 Byzantine Period
In AD 395, when Roman territory was divided, Greece fell within the Eastern Empire, then became part of the Byzantine Empire. By AD 389–393, philosophical schools were closed, pagan temples converted to churches and the Olympic Games suspended.

5 Ottoman Athens
The Ottoman Turks took Athens in 1456 from the Latin Catholic dukes, and the city became a provincial backwater. After bombarding the Parthenon, the Venetians held the city briefly in 1687. A few decades later, English and French artists began visiting Athens as part of the Grand Tour, aiding its rebirth, but also pilfering ancient artworks.

6 War of Independence
In 1821 Greeks rose against Ottoman domination – first alone, then with the aid of Britain, France and Russia. The war ended in 1829, but the Ottomans held the Acropolis until 1834, when King Otto I entered the city. Athens became capital of the new Greek state and was rebuilt, largely in Neo-Classical style.

Painting of the War of Independence

7 World War II

Mussolini declared war on Greece in October 1940, and the German army entered Athens on 23 April 1941, raising the swastika over the Acropolis. The Third Reich used the Hotel Grande Bretagne (see p144) as its wartime headquarters.

German planes during World War II

8 Post World War II

At the close of WWII, with its political future uncertain, Greece fell into civil war. The US began pouring economic and military aid into the country, to prevent the Communist rebels from taking power. In the 1950s and '60s, Athens saw rapid industrialization, mass migration from rural areas and the growth of sprawling suburbs.

9 Military Dictatorship

On 21 April 1967, a coup d'état led by Georgios Papadopoulos marked the beginning of a seven-year military junta. Student protests during mid-November 1973 were violently suppressed by the military, who stormed Athens' Polytechnic, killing many. The junta fell in July 1974.

10 Modern-Day Athens

Greece joined the EEC (now the EU) in 1981. In 1985, Athens was the first European Capital of Culture. The successful 2004 Olympics gave the city improved transport, sports and cultural facilities. However, since 2010 a chronic economic crisis has delivered harsh austerity, draconian currency controls, severe social unrest, frequent inconclusive elections and massive emigration.

TOP 10 ATHENIANS

1 Draco
In the 7th century BC, Draco instituted the first Code of Law: even trivial crimes incurred the death penalty, hence the term draconian.

2 Solon
Draco's laws were made less severe by Solon (c.638–559 BC). He also extended citizenship to the lower classes.

3 Kleisthenes
A statesman active around 508–506 BC, Kleisthenes replaced aristocratic rule with a democratic Assembly.

4 Themistokles
This general (c.524–459 BC) championed the navy as a force to expand the empire.

5 Perikles
Perikles (c.495–429 BC) beautified the city, let poorer citizens attend the Assembly, and extended the empire.

6 Aspasia
During the 5th century BC, this mistress of Perikles gained acceptance in Athens' male-dominated intellectual circles.

7 Demosthenes
The finest Greek orator (384–322 BC) overcame a speech impediment by talking with pebbles in his mouth.

8 Damaskinos
Archbishop of Athens from 1941, he defied the Nazi occupiers by issuing false baptismal certificates for Jews.

9 Dimitris Pikionis
Distinguished architect (1887–1968) who designed the 1950s stone walkways on the Acropolis' south slope.

10 Melina Mercouri
Much-loved actress (1920–94) who opposed the 1967–74 junta, became Minister of Culture and initiated the European Capital of Culture scheme.

The actress Melina Mercouri

TOP 10 Moments in the History of Theatre and Music

A modern production of *The Persians*, a play by Aeschylus

1 The Rites of Dionysos, 1200–600 BC

Annual rites to the god of wine and revelry were held each spring, and involved orgies, feasts and the ingestion of herbs that led to wild ecstasies. A dithyramb (ode to Dionysos) was sung by a chorus of men dressed as satyrs. It eventually evolved into narratives, which in turn developed into the first plays.

2 Thespis, 6th Century BC

During one of these group chorales, an intrepid performer named Thespis broke away from the group and added a solo narrative. The innovation took hold, and this new individual role became known as the protagonist, the individual hero of the drama, now backed by the chorus.

3 Drama Competitions, 534 BC

In 534 BC, the ruler of Athens, Peisistratos, formalized the Dionysian festivals into fully fledged drama competitions, held annually. Thespis won the first competition.

4 Aeschylus, the First Playwright, 472 BC

Aeschylus introduced a second character, the antagonist, creating new possibilities. In 472 BC came *The Persians*, the earliest known play.

5 Sophocles Beats Aeschylus in the Drama Competition, 468 BC

Sophocles brought another innovation to the form of drama: a third character. He also wrote what is still considered the greatest masterpiece of tragedy, *Oedipus Rex*.

6 Greek Shadow Puppet Theatre, 16th Century

After the Golden Age of Athenian drama, Greece's performing arts stagnated. However, during the Ottoman occupation, Greeks drew on an Eastern tradition of shadow puppet theatre. The stylized spectacles were satirical and bawdy, the main character (Karaghiozis the fool) joking at the expense of his social betters.

Greek shadow puppet

7 Rembetika Emerges, 1870s

When the Greeks threw off 400 years of Ottoman occupation, one of the first art forms to coalesce was rembetika, music that can be compared to the blues. Heavily influenced by music and instruments from Asia Minor, rembetika lyrics tell of life's underside: drugs, destitution, passion, exile and prison.

8 Maria Callas Dominates Opera, 1950s and 1960s

Born Maria Kalogeropoulou, the fiery first lady of opera was the original diva. She enraged many opera house managers with her whims, but she also seduced millions, including shipping magnate Aristotle Onassis, with her heavenly voice.

9 Mikis Theodorakis Writes the Songs of a Generation, 1960s and 1970s

Mikis Theodorakis, Greece's greatest modern composer, won international acclaim with works such as *Epiphania* and the instantly recognizable *Zorba the Greek* score. During the junta, Theodorakis's songs were banned and he was jailed, making him an instant symbol of the resistance.

A scene from *Chariots of Fire*

10 Vangelis's Chariots of Fire, 1981

Greek composer Vangelis won an Academy Award for his memorable score for *Chariots of Fire*, a film about Olympic runners. Vangelis is renowned for his electronic compositions and film scores, including the original *Bladerunner*.

TOP 10 THEATRE AND MUSIC VENUES

Odeon of Herodes Atticus

1 Odeon of Herodes Atticus
Entrance: MAP J5; Dionysiou Areopagitou ▪ Box office: MAP L/M2 ▪ www.greekfestival.gr
This huge amphitheatre (see p13) is the main venue for the Hellenic Festival.

2 Tivoli Live
MAP D2 ▪ Emmanouil Benaki 34 ▪ 210 383 0919
Stars such as Manolis Pappos and Yannis Niarhos play rembetika here (see p99).

3 National Opera
State-of-the-art Cultural Centre premises house this company (see p96).

4 National Theatre
Catch the National Theatre's classic performances here (see p96).

5 An Club
Rock, reggae and alternative music in the heart of Exárhia (see p99).

6 Gagarin 205
MAP B1 ▪ Liosion 205, Attiki metro ▪ 211 411 2500 ▪ www.gagarin25.gr
Great musicians often play at this venue.

7 Megaro Mousikis
MAP G3 ▪ Vas Sofias and Kokkali ▪ 210 728 2000 ▪ www.megaro.gr
Acoustics for the world's best orchestras, jazz bands and ballet companies.

8 Lykavittos Theatre
MAP F2 ▪ 210 722 7233
This theatre (see p102) showcases the best musical acts, from rock to classical.

9 Half Note
MAP M6 ▪ 210 921 3310 ▪ Trivonianou 17 ▪ www.halfnote.gr
Top-notch jazz musicians play here.

10 Epidauros
Tickets available from the Herodes Atticus or Panepistimiou box offices
Only ancient classics are performed in this famous amphitheatre (see p125).

TOP10 Archaeological Sites

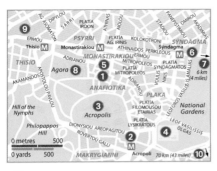

juxtaposition to the earlier archaeological finds within the museum (see p77).

3 Acropolis
If you're only in Athens for a day, this is the one sight to see (see pp12–13). The temples, especially the great Parthenon, built to honour Athena, have been a dominating influence in Western architecture for over 2,000 years. They continue to astonish and inspire.

1 Roman Forum and Tower of the Winds
One of the city's most interestingly layered sites (see pp24–5). Buildings and remains include the ingenious Tower of the Winds from 50 BC, the 1st-century AD Roman forum, and a well-restored Ottoman mosque.

The Roman Forum

2 Acropolis Museum
The museum (see pp14–15) has been built over a late-Roman and early Byzantine settlement. The site is packed with houses and at least one fountain and reservoir, rare in the parched city. A walkway through the site and glass floors in the museum allow visitors to see all angles of it, a fascinating

4 Temple of Olympian Zeus
The building of the colossal temple to Zeus (see pp36–7) was started in 515 BC and took nearly 700 years to complete, during which time many other buildings – temples, baths and a law court – sprang up around it.

5 Hadrian's Library
Hadrian built this luxurious Corinthian-columned building (see p84) in AD 132. Most of the space was a showy marble courtyard, with gardens and a pool. There were also lecture rooms, music rooms and a theatre. The library itself was on the east side, where you can see marble slots for manuscript scrolls.

6 Syndagma Metro Station
In the late 1990s, Athens undertook its biggest archaeological dig ever: excavating a long-delayed metro – essential for hosting the Olympics (see p101). Many feared that the tightly scheduled dig would endanger what lay beneath. The Syndagma metro station was a brilliant compromise: though modern and gleaming, one glass wall looks directly through to an archaeological site, with detailed explanations of its various layers.

statesmen hammered out the terms of the first democracy, was the city's heart and soul for 1200 years. This is one of the most hands-on sites in Athens and includes the Temple of Hephaistos, the best-preserved ancient Greek temple.

9 Kerameikos
This fascinating site *(see pp30–31)* around ancient Athens' walls should not be missed. It contains evidence of all the activities that take place at a city's edge: tombs (raised circular mounds for war heroes, pompous marble statues for great statesmen), temples, important roads, pottery workshops and a brothel. It's also a shady oasis in the congested city centre.

Kesariani monastery

7 Kesariani
MAP T2 ■ 210 723 6619
■ Open 8am–3pm Tue–Sun ■ Adm
This 11th-century monastery on the cypress-clad slopes of Mount Ymittos (the ancient Hymettos) makes a wonderful day trip (best reached by car). The chapel, *(see p46)* dedicated to the Presentation of the Theotokos, is built atop Classical ruins, and its walls are decorated with cloisonné (enamelled) masonry and late 17th-century paintings. The ram's-head fountain is said to cure infertility.

8 Agora
The Agora *(see pp16–17)*, the marketplace where philosophers held forth, tradesmen bickered and

10 Temple of Poseidon
MAP T3 ■ 70 km (43 miles) south of Athens on the Sounio Road ■ 229 203 9363 ■ Open summer: 9am–sunset daily (winter: from 9:30am) ■ Adm
The great marble shrine to the sea god, situated on Cape Sounio's summit and surrounded by the Aegean Sea, is among the most stunning sights in all of Greece. It was built in the early 5th century BC. British poet Lord Byron was one of many who fell under its spell 2,400 years later, composing poetry in its honour and carving his name on a pillar. Come at sunset, just before it closes, for a spectacular and unforgettable view.

Temple of Poseidon at Cape Sounio

TOP 10 Churches

1 Church of the Metamorphosis (Sotiros)

MAP C5 ■ Theorias St, Upper Plaka

This Byzantine church is situated on the northern slope of the Acropolis and dates back either to the second half of the 11th century or the 14th century. It is a four-columned church with a tall Athenian dome, typical of monuments from this period. The dome and the northern and southern sides have remained intact, but the western sides have been rebuilt.

2 Monastiraki

Once the greatest monastery of the area (see p86), this is the church from which the Monastiraki neighbourhood takes its name. "Little monastery" was so called after the destruction of its many surrounding buildings during 19th-century archaeological digs. The restored church itself is usually open.

3 Kesariani, Mount Ymittos

This 11th-century monastery (see p45) sits on fragrant, wooded slopes just outside Athens. Most of its surviving frescoes are from the 16th and 17th centuries, and its fountain waters that were said to cure infertility, are no longer drinkable.

4 Agii Apostoli

MAP J4

The Church of the Holy Apostles is one of Athens' oldest churches, built in the early 11th century over a 2nd-century monument in the ancient Agora. Though it suffered a great deal of damage during the Ottoman occupation, the remains of its frescoes have been preserved and restored within.

The 11th-century church, Agii Apostoli

Interior of Kapnikarea

5 Kapnikarea

This lovely little church *(see p87)*, dedicated to the Presentation of the Theotokos, was built in the 11th century over the ruins of an ancient temple. It is laid out in the typical Byzantine cross-in-square plan, with three apses on the east side and a narthex (a western portico). Inside, the church is decorated with frescoes by neo-Byzantinist Photis Kontoglou.

6 Panagia Grigoroussa/ Agios Fanourios

MAP J4 ■ Near Monastiraki Metro Station ■ Services Apr–Oct: 5:45pm; Nov–Mar: 4:45pm

If you've lost something, head to this church. Fanourios is the patron saint of lost objects. Every Saturday, the church conducts a liturgy blessing parishioners' *fanouropites* (cakes). Once eaten, it is believed that the lost object would reappear.

7 Agios Georgios

MAP P1

Claiming the highest point in modern-day Athens – the peak of Lykavittos Hill – Agios Georgios boasts views as far as the Saronic Gulf, the island of Egina and the Peloponnese coast. Services are held both inside and outside.

8 Panagia Gorgoepikoös

Dwarfed by the bulk of the modern Mitropoli, tiny Panagia Gorgoepikoös (Mikri Mitropoli, "little Cathedral") far outshadows its vast neighbour in historic and artistic importance *(see p79)*. It was built in the 12th century, on the ruins of an ancient temple dedicated to goddess Eileithyia. Its walls are built of Hellentistic, Roman and Byzantine marble relics, sculpted with reliefs depicting the ancient calendar of feasts.

9 Agia Ekaterini

Fragments of Classical columns remain in the courtyard of this beautiful 12th-century church *(see p80)* – it was built over the ruins of an ancient temple, possibly dedicated to the goddess Hestia. The church's colourful frescoes have been lovingly restored.

Religious art in Mitropoli

10 Mitropoli

Athens' massive cathedral *(see p79)* of 1862 was the first major church built after Greece's independence. It became the seat of the archbishop and hence of the established Greek state church. Though its colourful frescoes and pricey ecclesiastical objects are certainly impressive, its architecture is less so. Mitropoli's importance is almost entirely spiritual, as the focal point for the Greek Orthodox Church.

TOP 10 Museums

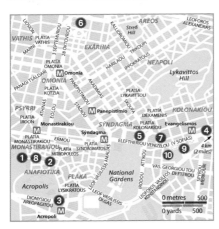

been filtered through the unique Hellenic sensibility. The array of beautiful instruments includes carved Byzantine lyres, ivory-inlaid lutes and pastoral flutes *(see p78)*.

3 Acropolis Museum

This beautiful museum *(see pp14–15)* was designed partly to provide a fitting home to the famed marble sculptures of the Acropolis, and partly as a political gambit to force Britain to return the Parthenon marbles, which currently reside in the British Museum.

1 Agora Museum

The fascinating displays of finds *(see pp18–19)* from the city's ancient marketplace focus on objects used in the workings of the first democracy, including the declaration inscribed on marble that a government of democracy, not tyranny, was to rule.

2 Museum of Greek Musical Instruments

Greek musical instruments are far more varied than the bouzouki that plucked out the theme to *Zorba the Greek*. The Greek musical tradition, though heavily influenced by Turkey and the Middle East, has

4 National Gallery of Art

■ Army Park in Goudi, Panagiotis Kanellopoulos Ave ■ Open 9am–6pm Mon–Thu ■ Closed Sun ■ Adm ■ www.nationalgallery.gr

Greece's most important art gallery, showcasing the masterpieces of Greek artists. Highlights of the collection include works by Greek Modernist Nikos Hatzikyriakou-Ghika and Neo-Byzantinist Photis Kontoglou, as well as 19th-century masters such as Nikiforos Lytras, Theodoros Vryzakis and Nikolaos Gyzis.

Display of bouzouki and lutes at the Museum of Greek Musical Instruments

5 Benaki Museum

Follow the progress of Greek art and culture through this first-rate collection from the eras of antiquity to the mid-20th century. Walk through excellently presented displays in the gorgeous Neo-Classical mansion *(see pp26–7)* of the Benaki family.

embroideries, costumes, shadow puppets and filigreed jewellery, from the mainland and the Aegean Islands. The collection also covers the renaissance of decorative crafts in the 18th and 19th centuries. The museum is currently closed and will reopen in Monastiraki in 2021.

Liturgical object at the Museum of Greek Folk Art

6 National Archaeological Museum

One of the world's most important museums *(see pp20–21)*, featuring a jaw-dropping array of treasures from the prehistoric and Classical Greek civilizations. Don't miss the exquisite frescoes of 17th-century-BC Thera, and the golden hoard of Bronze Age Mycenae.

National Archaeological Museum

7 Museum of Cycladic Art

The Cycladic island civilization of the Aegean flourished at the same time as the early Egyptians and Mesopotamians, but produced something very different: strangely elegant, stylized marble goddess-cult figurines *(see p102)*. These were the first pieces in the centuries-long tradition of Greek art that was to follow and this is the world's largest collection *(see pp22–3)*.

8 Museum of Greek Folk Art

A rich collection of Greek folk art *(see p78)* from 1650 to the present day, including traditional tapestries,

9 Byzantine and Christian Museum

Yet another of the top museums in the world *(see pp32–3)*. There are nearly 30,000 objects from Byzantine and post-Byzantine churches and monasteries across Greece, including sculpture, manuscripts, icons, frescoes and precious, eye-strainingly intricate gold, silver and gem-encrusted ecclesiastical objects.

10 War Museum

A lengthy display of warfare in Greece *(see p103)*, beginning with pre-historic battle-axes, running through Alexander the Great's battle plans and the Greek War of Independence to the present. The Saroglos collection includes medieval swords, Renaissance foils and duelling pistols, engraved Turkish scimitars and samurai blades. Unfortunately, the accompanying information is scarce and often only in Greek.

Exhibit at the War Museum

🔟 Philosophers and Writers

① Homer c.700 BC

Next to nothing is known about the bard who compiled the tales of *The Iliad* and *The Odyssey*. These poems, which were kept alive by oral tradition, are arguably the greatest and most influential in history.

② Aeschylus 535–456 BC

Homer

When the "Father of Tragedy" began writing, theatre was still in its infancy. Aeschylus brought a wealth of characters, powerful narratives, grandeur of language, and a sweeping vision of humans working out a plan of cosmic justice to works such as *Prometheus Unbound* and acclaimed trilogy *The Oresteia*.

③ Sophocles 496–406 BC

Only seven of Sophocles' plays survive, but his reputation rests securely on three: *Antigone*, *Oedipus at Kolonos* and *Oedipus Rex*. The last of these, the story of a king bound hopelessly by fate to murder his father and marry his mother, is considered the greatest masterpiece of Greek tragedy.

④ Socrates 470–399 BC

Though Socrates himself wrote nothing, his teachings, recorded in the writings of historians and especially his pupil Plato, have earned him the title of the forerunner of Western philosophy. At the height of the Golden Age of Athens, the original marketplace philosopher debated the great meanings in the Agora, and was eventually tried and put to death *(see p34)* for corrupting the youth of Athens.

⑤ Aristophanes 447–385 BC

The greatest comic playwright of Greece brought a welcome breath of fresh air and levity after the age of the great tragedians. Aristophanes' raunchy, hilarious *Lysistrata*, in which the women of warring Sparta and Athens refuse to sleep with their husbands until they stop fighting, remains one of the greatest anti-war messages of all time.

⑥ Plato 428–348 BC

If Socrates was the forerunner of Western philosophy, then Plato was its foundation. His works – from his early dialogues reprising Socrates' teachings, to later masterworks such as the seminal *Republic* – comprised the backbone of every major intellectual movement to follow.

Plato and Aristotle, as portrayed by Raphael in *The School of Athens*

⑦ Aristotle 384–322 BC

After studying with Plato, Aristotle tutored Alexander the Great. He later set up the Lykeio, a competitor to Plato's Academy. His *Poetics* is still one of the most

Aristotle tutoring Alexander the Great

important works of literary criticism, and his *Nichomachean Ethics* is among the greatest treatises on ethics.

8 Nikos Kazantzakis 1883–1957

Many have been drawn to the strange, joyous, bittersweet spirit of modern Greece, as depicted in Kazantzakis' most famous work, *Zorba the Greek*. Darker in mood is *The Last Temptation of Christ*, and best of all is his autobiographical *Report to Greco*, which among other things chronicles his childhood in Ottoman Crete.

9 George Seferis 1900–71

Greece's first Nobel Laureate was born in Smyrna, which fell to modern Turkey in 1922, and his lyrical poetry is inspired by history and feelings of exile. His work also relates Greece's Classical past to its raw present, as in *Mythistorema*, a series of poems that draws from *The Odyssey*.

10 Yanis Varoufakis b.1961

Challenging EU austerity measures while serving as Finance Minister in the left-wing Syriza government in 2015, Varoufakis stood out for being outspoken. This academic, economist and game-theory expert chronicled his experiences in the books *The Weak Suffer What They Must?* and *Adults in the Room*.

TOP 10 TOMES

1 *The Iliad*, Homer
One small episode in the Trojan War, told in the greatest epic ever written.

2 *The Odyssey*, Homer
Detailing Odysseus's adventures with sirens, nymphs and Kyklops as he makes his way from Troy back home to the island of Ithaca.

3 *The Oresteia*, Aeschylus
Brilliant trilogy about the House of Atreus, the most dysfunctional family in ancient Greece.

4 *The Theban Tragedies*, Sophocles
Terrible events unfold when Oedipus kills his father and marries his mother. A dramatic text to read on a visit to Delphi and Thebes.

5 *The Republic*, Plato
Still the blueprint for the best way to run a government.

6 *Constitution of Athens*, Aristotle
A work that marries the democratic political structure of Athens with the architectural structure of the Agora.

7 *History of the Peloponnesian War*, Thucydides
Month-by-month, blow-by-blow historical account of the conflict by an Athenian officer.

8 *The Histories*, Herodotus
Compelling reportage of the Greeks' fight for freedom against the Persians, as told by the "Father of History".

9 *The Guide to Greece*, Pausanias
Pausanias, arguably the world's first travel writer, recorded observations from all over Greece during his 2nd-century AD journey.

10 *Zorba the Greek*, Nikos Kazantzakis
Rose to fame as a modern Greek novel after a film was made on it in 1964.

Anthony Quinn in *Zorba the Greek*

⏨ Athenian Legends

Painting depicting the story of Theseus killing the Minotaur

1 Theseus Kills the Minotaur

Upon the death of his son in Athens, Minos, King of Crete, demanded the King of Athens, Aegeas, send regular tributes of 14 youths and maidens, who were sacrificed to the monstrous Minotaur. One year, Theseus was sent and, with the help of Minos's daughter, Ariadne, he killed the Minotaur, saving hundreds of future Athenians.

2 The Birth of Erichthonios

Hephaistos tried to rape Athena, but only managed to spill his seed on her leg. Athena brushed it to the ground, where it turned into an infant with the help of the earth-goddess Gaia. Athena entrusted the daughters of King Kekrops to raise the child. After he grew up Erichthonios assumed the throne.

The Birth of Erichthonios

3 The Birth of Athena

Zeus was told that his pregnant mistress Metis would have a son who would dethrone him. To prevent this, he swallowed Metis whole, but the unborn child continued to grow in Zeus's head. After nine months, Hephaistos split open the god's head with an axe, and out sprang the fully grown goddess Athena, in complete armour.

4 The Naming of Athens

Athena and Poseidon, god of the sea, competed for patronage of the city by offering useful gifts. Poseidon struck his trident into the rock of the Acropolis and out gushed salt water. Athena offered the olive tree, and the city was awarded to her.

5 Theseus's Arrival in Athens

Theseus, son of King Aegeas, was raised far from court in Troezen. At 16, wielding his father's sword, Theseus left for Athens, en route slaying six bandits or monsters terrorizing Attica. He became Athens' greatest king.

6 The Rape of Philomela

Pandion had two daughters, Prokne and Philomela. When the former's husband Tereas raped Philomela and cut out her tongue, Prokne took revenge by serving the flesh of their son to Tereas. The gods then made Prokne into a swallow, Tereas into a hoopoe and Philomela into a nightingale (which cries "Tereu").

7 The Trial of Orestes

After murdering his mother, Klytemnestra (to avenge her murder of his father, Agamemnon), Orestes was pursued to Athens by the Furies (goddesses of vengeance). Athena decreed that, instead of being killed, Orestes should stand trial. The trial marked a turning point in Athens, from blood feuds to rule of law.

8 Athena and Arachne

As goddess of spinning, Athena decided to help a poor but talented weaver called Arachne. Arachne won great admiration but never credited the goddess, so Athena challenged her to a weaving contest. Arachne's work depicted the inappropriate love affairs of the gods; Athena, indignant at this disrespect, turned Arachne into the first spider.

Athena and Arachne

9 The Death of Aegeas

Theseus had told his father that if he succeeded in killing the Minotaur, he would change his ship's sails from black to white. But, after all the excitement, he forgot. Upon seeing the black sails, Aegeas was stricken with grief and plunged to his death in the sea (now the Aegean).

10 Perseus Kills Medusa

Perseus was the son of Zeus and the maiden Danae. The king of Seriphos, Polydektes, desired Danae, but Perseus promised him the snake-infested head of Medusa in exchange for his mother's safety. Perseus slew Medusa with Athena's help, then turned Polydektes to stone.

TOP 10 GODS AND MONSTERS

1 Zeus
The Pantheon's supreme god ruled the skies and fathered hundreds of heroes with his superhuman libido.

2 Poseidon
The god of the sea was Zeus's brother – and sometimes his greatest rival.

3 Athena
Zeus's daughter was a virgin warrior goddess of wisdom and crafts. She was also goddess of weaving and patron of Athens.

4 Medusa
The gaze of this snake-headed gorgon turned men to stone. Perseus killed her with the help of Athena's gleaming shield, in which he could safely see his foe.

5 Artemis
Apollo's twin sister was goddess of the moon, wild animals and the hunt, and remained a virgin.

6 Aphrodite
Voluptuous Aphrodite was Artemis's polar opposite – the temperamental goddess of love had dozens of affairs.

7 The Minotaur
Crete's Queen Pasiphae conceived this bull-headed, human-bodied monster with a bull sent by Poseidon.

8 The Kykopes
The most famous of these one-eyed giants is Polyphemos, the monstrous son of Poseidon whom Odysseus blinded in Homer's *The Odyssey*.

9 The Sirens
The beautiful sirens with their bewitching songs nearly lured Odysseus's sailors to their deaths on a rocky shore.

10 Apollo
The handsome god of music and poetry presided over the Muses.

Statue of the god Apollo

🔟 Greek Inventions

The archaeological site at Olympia

1 Olympic Games
The first recorded games were staged on the plains of Olympia in 776 BC. Dedicated to Zeus, they lasted one day and featured running and wrestling. In 648 BC – with the addition of boxing, the *pankration* (another form of hand-to-hand combat), horse racing and the pentathlon (sprinting, long-jump, javelin, discus and wrestling) – the event was extended to five days and held every four years.

2 Athenian Trireme
Masterpieces of ancient shipbuilding (700–400 BC), triremes were the key to Athens' naval strength. Approximately 40 m (130 ft) long and 5 m (16 ft) wide, they were noted for great speed – up to 12 knots. The boats were powered by 170 oarsmen seated on three tiers. Only one tier rowed at a time, alternating short shifts so that they did not exhaust themselves all at once. The vessels were also equipped with sails, which were lowered during battle.

3 Theatre
The earliest form of theatre can be traced back to an ancient Greek pagan ritual, which developed into an annual drama competition in the 6th century BC (see p42). Plays were performed outside in daylight in purpose-built amphitheatres, and actors wore a range of masks to indicate different characters. The oldest plays emphasize values such as Greek patriotism, reverence to the gods, liberty and hospitality.

4 Pythagoras's Theorem
"The square of the hypotenuse of a right-angled triangle is equal to the sum of the squares of the other two sides." This theorem, discovered by the philosopher and mathematician Pythagoras (570–495 BC) was a major scientific breakthrough, which led to extraordinary advances in mathematics, geometry and astronomy.

5 Democracy
Demokratia ("rule of the people") as a form of government was first introduced in Athens under Kleisthenes in 508–506 BC. All free, male, adult citizens of Athenian birth were entitled to attend the Assembly – which met on the Pnyx Hill – and thus participate in political decision-making. The Assembly gathered about 40 times a year, and 6,000 citizens needed to be present to make a vote valid.

6 Hippocratic Oath
Attributed to Hippocrates, the Greek physician and the father of medicine (460–375 BC), this oath prohibits doctors from performing unnecessary surgery, abortions or euthanasia. It requires them to abstain from sexual relations with patients, and to keep information divulged to them confidential. The oath was taken by doctors until 1948, when the World Medical Association created a modern restatement called the Declaration of Geneva.

7 Catapult
Invented by Dionysios the Elder of Syracuse (c.430–367 BC), the catapult can hurl heavy objects or shoot arrows over large distances. Having seized power in Sicily, Dionysios set about driving out the Carthaginians, who ruled a large part of the island. Thanks in part to the catapult, he was successful, making Syracuse the strongest power in Greek Italy.

The Romans later perfected his invention, adding wheels to catapults to make them mobile.

8 Greek Fire

Used as a secret weapon by the Byzantine Empire against enemy ships, Greek Fire was a highly flammable, jelly-like substance. It was blasted through bronze tubes mounted on the prows of Byzantine galleys, and was inextinguishable by water. It was first employed to repel an Arab fleet attacking Constantinople in 673, and then successfully used in combat until the late 12th century. Scientists are still unsure of its exact formula but think that it consisted of liquid petroleum, sulphur, naphtha and quicklime.

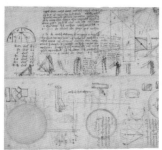

Leonardo da Vinci's sketch of Archimedes' Screw

9 Archimedes' Screw

The Syracusan-born Greek mathematician Archimedes (287–212 BC) invented an ingenious water pump, which became known as Archimedes' screw. It consisted of a tube coiled around a rod, which is set at an angle, with the bottom end in water and a handle at the top. When the handle is rotated, the entire device turns and the tube collects water which is thus transported upwards.

10 Pap Smear

Since 1943, cervical cancer has been detected using the Pap smear test, a gynaecological procedure named after its inventor, the Athens-educated Greek-American doctor, George Papanikolaou (1883–1962).

TOP 10 OLYMPIC FACTS

1 Decline of the Ancient Olympics
In AD 392–93, the Christian Emperor Theodosios I banned all 'pagan' observances, including the Olympics.

2 Revival of the Olympics
After 1,500 years the games were revived with the efforts of French Baron Pierre de Coubertin (1863–1937).

3 The First Modern Olympic Games
The first modern games were held in Athens, during April 1896 at the Kallimarmaro stadium.

5 The Olympic Rings
The five interlocking coloured rings represent the continents. It was designed by Baron de Coubertin in 1912.

6 The Olympic Medal
The last Olympic gold medals to be made entirely out of gold were awarded in 1912.

7 The Olympic Motto
The motto– *Citius, Altius, Fortius* (Swifter, Higher, Stronger) – was borrowed by Baron de Coubertin in 1921, from his late friend Henri Didon, a Dominican friar.

8 The Games Grow
The games took off as an international event in 1924, with the 8th Olympiad held in Paris.

4 The Olympic Flame
In 1936, Carl Diem started the tradition whereby a torch ignited in Greece was transported by relay to the host city, and kept alight until the Games ended.

9 The First Olympic TV Broadcast
The 1936 Berlin Summer Olympic games were the first to be covered live on television.

10 The Second Modern Greek Games
In 2004, the Summer Olympics returned to Athens for the first time since 1896.

Summer Olympics in 2004, Athens

🔟 Artistic Styles

1 Cycladic, 3200–2000 BC

The prehistoric Cycladic civilization flourished on the islands of Naxos, Paros, Amorgos, Milos, Syros and Keros (which form a rough circle around the holy island of Delos) for over 1,000 years, before mysteriously disappearing. It left behind hundreds of marble figures: most are elegant, angular, minimalist female figures, probably used in a funerary or fertility cult.

Angular Cycladic figurine

2 Minoan, 2000–1400 BC

The Minoans of Crete were sensual, social, nature-loving and matri-archal. Ceramics are painted with flowing lines based on natural motifs. Fluid-lined frescoes depict priestesses, bull-vaulting and animals. Most exciting are the faïence sculptures of voluptuous goddesses wielding snakes, and the fantastically light, delicate gold jewellery.

3 Mycenaean, 1600–1100 BC

The art of this martial mainland culture was somewhat influenced by the Minoans. But they were fundamentally different, focused on war, order and acquisition, especially of gold. Their palaces housed hoards of embossed-gold swords, daggers, and cups, gold death-masks and pots painted with warrior images.

4 Geometric, 9th–7th Century BC

Geometric art emerged from a dark age with vases painted with angular designs, and abstract, triangular-rectilinear human forms. The giant 8th-century BC funerary vase in the National Archaeological Museum is iconic, where you can see the first "Greek key" pattern.

Admiring Archaic sculptures

5 Archaic, Mid-7th–Early 5th Century BC

The start of monumental Greek art, with the first marble temples and sculptures. Early statues of young men and women, called *kouroi and korai respectively*, and made for religious purposes, were heavily influenced by Egyptian art: stiff, with carved and brightly painted garments and facial features.

6 Classical, 480–323 BC

The advent of naturalistic sculptures balancing vibrancy and idealism. Temples were built according to mathematical proportions, adorned with tradition-shattering sculptural reliefs that seemed to break out from the marble. Many were created by the sculptor Pheidias, a central figure of Athens' Golden Age.

Reconstructed Mycenaean fresco

7 Hellenistic, 323 BC–1st Century AD

Classical sculpture grew ripe and decadent, in part influenced by the new Hellenistic cities in the Orient, founded by Alexander the Great or his successors. The sculptor Lysippos defined the new phase with sensuous subjects such as Aphrodite, Pan and Dionysos in exaggerated, twisting movement.

14th-century Byzantine icon

8 Byzantine, c. 330–1500

Byzantine art was almost completely focused on depicting Christian images. Rich, colourful mosaics, frescoes, icons and religious objects were made with valuable materials, especially gold, and using intricate methods, which conveyed the wealth of the empire.

9 Ottoman Influence, 1453–1821

Under Islamic rule, monumental and public art was restricted, but folk arts flourished, incorporating aspects from the conqueror's culture, including intricate silver jewellery, metalwork, rugs, tapestries and embroideries.

10 Neo-Classical, 1836–Early 20th Century

The artistic tastes of independent Greece were determined by the Bavarian and Danish royal court and its architects, who were inspired by the Classical Greek monuments. Many of modern Athens' most important buildings were constructed on this model, notably the University of Athens, the Academy of Athens and the National Library.

TOP 10 ARTISTIC TERMS

1 Kouros/Kore
The first monumental sculptures in Greek art: a *kouros* was a youth, a *kore* a maiden. The plurals are *kouroi* and *korai* respectively.

2 Capital
The top of a column. There are three main Greek forms: Doric, a simple slab; Ionic, a carved scroll; and Corinthian, with an acanthus-leaf pattern.

3 Icon
Byzantine images of saints, believed to have holy power. They are often painted on a gold-leaf base.

4 Pediment
The triangular gable supported by columns on the temple's façade; often features relief sculptures.

5 Frieze
Horizontal band below the pediment of a temple, carved with decorative motifs.

6 Krater
A large ceramic or bronze bowl, often beautifully decorated, used for mixing wine and water.

7 Black-Figure Pottery
The earliest type of Greek vase-painting, etched into red ceramic glaze, creating a somewhat stiff, formal image.

8 Red-Figure Pottery
A revolutionary method of Classical vase-painting. The outlines of figures are painted on with red glaze, creating flowing, active images.

9 Fresco
A painting made directly upon the plaster before it has dried, creating art that is integral to the wall.

10 Caryatids
Sculptures of women used as columns. The most famous are at the Erechtheion at the Acropolis.

Caryatids at the Erechtheion

Following pages Walkway at Athens' Olympic site

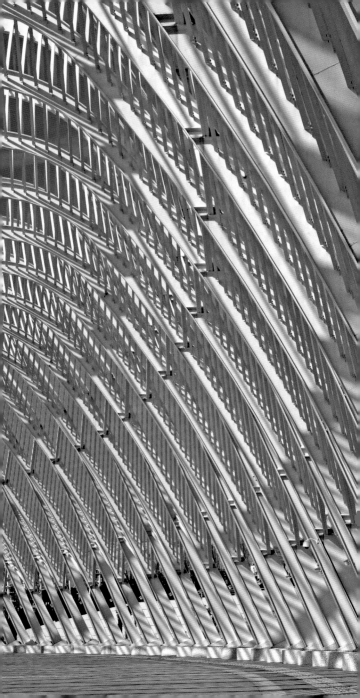

🔟 City Strolls

Ermou, Athens' main shopping street

1 Ermou

This is Athens' most popular shopping street. Start at the top, with designer boutiques and department stores. Make your way down to the funkier end, where flea markets *(see p87)* are set up adjacent to the street. Beyond it are quirky used-furniture, antiques and speciality shops.

2 Dionysiou Areopagitou Walkway

A continuous pedestrian link between all the major archaeological sites in central Athens, this wide, tree-lined walkway has several open-air cafés.

3 Kallidromiou and Strefi Hill

Kallidromiou is the heart of Exárhia, especially on Saturdays, when the whole neighbourhood turns out for the open-air *laiki agora* (farmer's market). Soak up the sights of the street and buy some fresh fruit before heading to nearby Strefi Hill *(see p95)* for a healthy climb and bite to eat.

4 Philopappos Hill

Follow the winding paths to different monuments including two historic churches, a Roman memorial and Athens' old observatory. At the summit of this shady hill *(see pp34–5)*, enjoy extensive views over and beyond the city.

5 First National Cemetery of Athens

MAP D–E6

Take a contemplative walk through the wide, overgrown rows of handsome mausoleums in Athens' largest cemetery. It is thickly planted with cypress trees, whose tall, pointed shape the Greeks believe helps to guide souls up to heaven.

6 Lykavittos Hill

Several pleasant footpaths run through pine-clad Lykavittos Hill *(see p102)*. If you're feeling energetic, hike to the top; if climbing's not for you, take the funicular up and saunter down, stopping at the café for a drink.

Walking up Lykavittos Hill, overlooking the city

7 Zea (Pasalimani)

This natural harbour (see p109) at Piraeus is full of local fishing boats and yachts. Stroll around the marina, ending up on the west side, in front of the Nautical Museum, or come after dark when the many waterside cafés come to life.

8 Kallimarmaro Stadium

Ancient Panathenaic athletes and the runners of the first modern Olympics in 1896 ran laps in the sweltering centre of this beautiful marble stadium (see p101). Modern joggers and walkers love the shady path on top of the 70,000-seat edifice. It is also used for concerts and rallies.

National Gardens

9 National Gardens

The winding paths of the lush National Gardens (see p101) are a great place for a stroll. Started in 1839, this was a royal park, and the landscape was densely planted with 15,000 exotic trees and flowers imported from around the world; many of those original plants still flourish.

10 Flisvos Marina

For a taste of cosmopolitan Athens, head to Flisvos Marina, where some of the most impressive yachts in the Mediterranean dock. A stroll along the promenade takes you past an outdoor shopping centre plus restaurants and cafés with sea views.

TOP 10 CITY VIEWS

City as seen from Areopagos rock

1 Areopagos
This high, slippery rock jutting over the Agora is where, for centuries, Athens' ruling council met.

2 Orizontes Restaurant
Watch the glittering nighttime cityscape from Orizontes (see p107) on Lykavittos Hill.

3 Philopappos Monument
Spectacular views directly across to the temples of the Acropolis or to Piraeus and the coast (see p34).

4 Adrianou, Monastiraki
Sit in one of the many outdoor cafés lining this street (see p88) for a ring-side view of the ancient marketplace.

5 360 Cocktail Bar
A classic Monastiraki rooftop bar and café with prime views of the Acropolis.

6 Galaxy Bar
A popular spot (see p106) for the fashionable set, the bar on the top floor of the Hilton Hotel offers stunning views over Athens in the evening.

7 Strefi Hill
In the shadow of Lykavittos, this green hill (see p95) is perfect if you desire a shorter climb but comparable views.

8 Athens Tower Mesogeion 2
Greece's tallest building; no observation deck, but great views if you're visiting any of its companies.

9 Kesariani Monastery
Lovely monastery on the wooded slopes of Mount Hymettos, above Athens' eastern suburbs (see p45).

10 Mount Pendeli
Up by the Astronomical Station in Athens' northernmost suburb, you get a great view of the city – day or night.

🔟 Off the Beaten Track

1 The Breeder Gallery

MAP B2 ■ Iasonos 45, Metaxourgio ■ noon–6pm Tue–Sat ■ www. thebreedersystem.com

West of Omonia, the up-and-coming (if somewhat seedy) neighbourhood of Metaxourgio is home to a growing number of art galleries, museums and trendy restaurants and cafés. Since 2008, the oldest and best-known gallery here, The Breeder, showcases contemporary art. It promotes emerging Greek talent as well as exhibits works by established international artists.

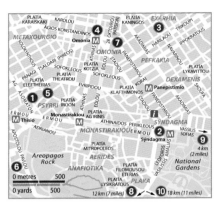

2 City Streets & Great Eats

MAP C4 ■ Meet at Syndagma Square ■ Open from 10am Mon–Sat ■ Reservations essential ■ www. alternativeathens.com

Revealing local shopping haunts, this 5- to 6-hour tour, run by Alternative Athens, takes you to family-run food stores and delicatessens around Monastiraki and Psyrri, as well as the Central Market. Arrive hungry – there's lots of tasting along the way.

A stop on the food walk

3 Grigoropoulos Shrine

MAP D2 ■ Tzavella, Exárhia

Commemorating 15-year-old Alexandros Grigoropoulos, who was killed here by the police in 2008, this small shrine lies on a pedestrianized alley in bohemian Exárhia. Marked by a marble plaque, flickering candles and flowers, it is a gathering point for left-wing students and anarchists.

4 Athens Street Art

MAP C2 ■ Gazi, Psyrri & Keramikos ■ Open from 10am daily ■ Reservations essential ■ www. alternativeathens.com

Athens is known for its graffiti artists, who make political statements with colour and humour on walls around the city. This three-hour tour takes you through the edgy neighbourhoods of Gazi, Metaxourgio and Psyrri, to reveal some of the city's most impressive graffiti.

5 Alibi Gallery

MAP B3 ■ Sarri 12, Psyrri ■ 10:30am–10pm Wed–Mon ■ www.alibigallery.com

Founded in 2013, this cutting-edge gallery features works by top local and international artists. They also encourage pop-up street-art events.

6 Cine Thision

MAP B5 ■ Apostolou Pavlou 7, Thisio ■ Open early May–late Oct, screenings 9pm & 11pm ■ Adm ■ www.cine-thisio.gr

Hidden behind a wall, between the Pnyx and the Areopagos, Athens' oldest *therinos* (open-air summer cinema) dates from 1935. Locals flock here for outdoor films on balmy evenings. There's a bar for drinks and a magical view of the floodlit Acropolis. The vintage or recent films are in their original version, with Greek subtitles.

7 Culinary Secrets of Downtown Athens

MAP K3 ■ Meet at Platía Omonia ■ Open from 9:30am & 1pm Mon–Sat ■ Reservations recommended ■ www.culinarybackstreets.com

This walking-and-tasting tour lasts for five-and-a-half hours. It explores hidden eateries in central Athens and regional dishes ranging from Macedonian-style *souvlaki* to Cretan recipes. Tastings are included in the fee.

8 Glyfada Beach

MAP T3 ■ Glyfada, 12 km (7.5 miles) from Athens, Attica coast ■ May–Oct ■ Adm

Few European capitals have beaches so close to the city centre. The tram from Syndagma takes you directly to Glyfada, a residential suburb with a sandy beach. In summer, locals arrive during their lunch break, take a dip, then go back to work. Stunning sunsets too.

Glyfada Beach

9 Kesariani Monastery

MAP T2 ■ Kesariani ■ 210 723 6619 ■ 8am–3pm Tue–Sun ■ Adm

A 25-minute bus ride from Syndagma, followed by a short walk up the lower slopes of Mount Ymittos, brings you to this originally 11th-century Orthodox monastery, set amid unspoilt nature. There's a Byzantine church with lovely frescoes, plus the ruins of the refectory, monks' cells and a bathhouse. It is occasionally visited by tour groups, but it mostly remains deserted.

Kesariani Monastery

10 Spa at the Divani Apollon Palace & Thalasso

MAP T3 ■ Agiou Nikolaou 10, Vouliagmeni ■ 210 891 1100 ■ 10am–10pm Mon–Fri, 10am–8pm Sat, 11am–7pm Sun ■ www.divani apollonthalasso.com

For relaxation and revitalization, visit Athens' largest spa, on the coast at Vouliagmeni. Centred on an indoor seawater pool with underwater jets, it offers beauty treatments, a range of massages, hammam, sauna and an ultra-modern gym.

🔟 Greek Dishes

1 Moussakas
There are endless variations on this famous country casserole, but the basic ingredients – aubergine and minced lamb layered with potatoes and tomatoes, enriched with wine, spiced with nutmeg and topped with bechamel – stay the same. The flavour is warming and earthy.

2 Kouneli Stifado
This rich, tender wild rabbit stew comes from the mountains of northern Greece, where it still warms villagers every winter. The rabbit is spiced with tomatoes or vinegar, garlic and cinnamon, but its most wonderful characteristic is an unusual sweetness, achieved by the addition of dessert wine and lots of small onions, cooked until caramelized.

3 Horiatiki
A bastardized version appears on menus worldwide as "Greek salad". The real thing is just a matter of fresh ingredients. Sun-ripened tomatoes, crisp cucumbers, fiery red onions and green peppers, rich Kalamata olives, topped with a slab of feta, aromatic oregano or savoury vinegar, and extra-virgin olive oil make up this simple but soothing salad.

Grilled octopus

4 Grilled Octopus
Best caught and served on the same day, having been grilled over hot coals, topped with oregano and drizzled with oil and vinegar. The texture should be tender and the taste salty-sweet.

Stifado, or rabbit stew

5 Pites
Pites came to Greece from Turkey and the Middle East. The key to perfect *pites* (which means "pies") is the famous phyllo crust: dozens of layers of paper-thin, translucent dough, brushed with butter or olive oil and baked to light, flaky perfection. Fillings range from sweet (the honey, walnut and rosewater baklava) to savoury – spinach and feta or *hortopita*, made from wild greens.

6 Kokoretsi
EU food laws concerning offal have made this backcountry dish technically illegal, but in secluded gardens and old-time tavernas Greeks continue to serve it on the sly. Intestines of lamb are marinated in herbs, garlic and lemon juice, wrapped carefully around a spit and roasted for hours over coals, until it drips with flavourful juices.

Horiatiki

7 Gemista

The name simply means "stuffed". Greeks pack tomatoes, aubergines, courgettes (zucchini), peppers and cabbage leaves with all manner of ingredients, including rice, herbs, raisins, pine nuts and an array of spices. The stuffed grape leaves are called *dolmadakia* or *yaprakia*.

8 Fasolada

The staple winter dish for the ancient Greeks, *fasolada* is still Greece's most popular soup. White beans, carrots, onions, celery and paprika are simmered in stock until tender, then topped with the crucial ingredient: extra-virgin olive oil. In summer, cold *fasolada* may be served as a meze in the afternoon.

Souvlaki on a bed of vegetables

9 Souvlaki

Souvla means a roasting spit, and this is the Greeks' favourite way to prepare meat. *Souvlaki* refers to the ubiquitous street favourite: bits of chicken, pork or lamb spit-roasted for hours. They are often basted with *tzatziki* (yogurt dip), and stuffed along with onions and tomatoes into a hot, freshly baked, oiled and fried pita bread.

10 Spetzofaï

Originating from Mount Pilion in Thessaly, this quick fry-up of sausages, aubergine, peppers and spices is a common dish and is found everywhere in Greece. There is a considerable amount of variation in this dish as each locale makes its own kind of sausages.

TOP 10 GREEK DRINKS

Ouzo

1 Ouzo
Greece wouldn't be the same without this spirit. Drunk with *mezedes* (snacks), this aniseed-flavoured distillate can be up to 47% alcohol.

2 Tsipouro
Similar to ouzo, this warm mainland drink is made from grape pomace left over from wine-making. Best for winters.

3 Retsina
The taste is not subtle, but affection for this wine with pine-resin-flavoured wine cuts across all age and class barriers.

4 Hyma (Bulk) Wine
Wine poured into tin measuring cups of glass flagons, preferably from barrels.

5 Dessert Wines
There are several noteworthy sweet fortified wines such as muscat-based white wine or the dark mavrodaphne.

6 Agiorgitiko Red Wines
"St George" grapes, usually from Nemea are the basis for some of the most popular, velvety Greek red wines.

7 Assyrtiko White Wines
Greece's star white grape – usually grown in Santorini but also found in Macedonia – is redolent of honeysuckle and figs.

8 Raki/Souma
Island favourites, raki and souma are other distillates made from either grape pomace or figs.

9 Greek Coffee
Powdered robusta beans are boiled in a long-handled *briki* (copper pot) and sweetened to taste.

10 Frappé
Instant coffee, milk, chipped ice and cold water whipped into a pleasant, cool froth.

Restaurants

1 Cookoovaya

This experimental restaurant *(see p107)* brings together five noted Greek chefs in a modern, open-plan kitchen. Try the beef carpaccio with gorgonzola sauce, or the octopus with fava bean purée.

Elegant dining at Cookoovaya

2 Manas Kouzina-Kouzina

Set in a historic square with views of the Acropolis, Manas Kouzina-Kouzina ("mother's kitchen") *(see p90)* specializes in regional Greek dishes such as Naxos-style pork neck or sea-bass fillet with vegetables and celery-root purée.

3 Funky Gourmet, Keramikos-Metaxourgio

Serving degustation menus with selected wine pairings (no à la carte), the Michelin-starred Funky Gourmet *(see p90)* specializes in molecular gastronomy based on Mediterranean ingredients. Dinner here is a real event in itself – theatrical, sensual and full of surprises.

4 Varoulko Seaside, Mikrolimano, Piraeus

Celebrity chef Lefteris Lazarou serves creative seafood dishes at waterside tables overlooking Mikrolimano *(see p112)*. Dishes such as grilled squid with black-eyed beans, marjoram and cumin, and oven-baked John Dory with cauliflower purée have earned him a Michelin star.

5 Mani Mani

Greek-American brothers add international style and a delicate, inspired touch to the cuisine here *(see p83)*. Menu highlights include pork tenderloin with soft cheese, figs, honey and almonds, or chickpeas with cumin, cabbage and fresh mint.

6 Milos

Costas Spiliadis, founder of eponymous sister restaurants in New York, Las Vegas, Miami, Montreal and London, also has a branch in Athens' Hilton Hotel *(see p107)*. Expect impeccable service and exquisite Greek seafood dishes in a luxurious setting. They offer a tasting menu for lunch as well as à la carte.

7 Aleria, Metaxourgio

A fine choice for a romantic dinner for two, Aleria *(see p90)* serves tasty contemporary cuisine, with favourites such as mixed-greens phyllo pie, and couscous *bourdeto* (Corfiot fish stew) with scorpion fish, mussels and squid. To try several dishes, opt for one of the reasonably priced five- or seven-course tasting menus.

Romantic setting at Aleria

Two Michelin-starred Spondi

8 Spondi

The most sophisticated restaurant *(see p107)* in Athens boasts two Michelin stars and offers exquisitely prepared and presented haute cuisine by chef Angelos Lantos. Try dishes such as crab with turnip, honey, tarragon and passiflora, or venison in Sarawak pepper crust.

Hytra, Onassis Cultural Centre

9 Hytra

Michelin-starred chef Tassos Mantis serves spectacularly prepared and presented food *(see p83)*. There is an excellent eight-course degustation menu. Try the freshwater crayfish in basil and wild garlic sauce or the sea bass cooked with potato-leek cream and saffroned baby onions.

10 Orizontes

Perched on Lykavittos Hill, Orizontes *(see p107)* is an unforgettable dining venue. The city views are stunning, and the creative Mediterranean cuisine and extensive wine list are both excellent.

TOP 10 TAVERNAS

1 Klimataria
This historic taverna *(see p98)* is popular with locals due to its rembetika music, dancing and excellent dishes.

2 Nikitas
Excellent value *magirefta* (slow-cooked food) with decent bulk wine and friendly service *(see p90)*.

3 Filippou
Old-world taverna *(see p103)* in Athens' poshest neighbourhood. Specializes in Greek casseroles as well as grills and fish dishes.

4 Bakaliarakia tou Damigou
An underground hideaway *(see p83)* with justly famous fried cod and its very own ancient column.

5 Yiantes
Enjoy a variety of Greek dishes prepared with mainly organic ingredients in a pretty walled courtyard *(see p98)*.

6 To Kafenion
Delicious traditional food is served in cosy surroundings *(see p83)*.

7 Mouries
This traditional taverna *(see p107)*, serves excellent steam-trays. There are outdoor tables under mulberry trees.

8 Ama Lachei
MAP D1 ▪ Kallidromiou 69
▪ 210 384 5978 ▪ €
Set in a quiet corner, this taverna has a cosy wooden-floored interior, with summer tables in its tiered garden.

9 Thanassis
The house special here *(see p90)* is beef-based, spicy Egyptian style kebab.

10 Rififi
A contemporary taverna *(see p98)* with a summery pastel-hued decor. Lots for vegetarians, and good choice of beers and Greek distillates.

Relaxed and fun Rififi

For a key to restaurant price ranges see p83

☒10 **Places to Shop**

1 Folli Follie

Now a major player with more than 600 retail outlets worldwide, Folli Follie *(see p105)* was established in Greece in 1982. Fashion-conscious women flock to this store in search of accessories such as jewellery, watches, bags and belts. The philosophy behind the brand is affordable luxury.

2 Loumidis Coffee Shop

The oldest surviving coffee roaster in Greece *(see p97)*. This caffeine-fancier's paradise stocks a wealth of traditional Greek coffees, plus all the paraphernalia necessary for its preparation. It also sells a range of beans from around the world, as well as espresso machines, cups, shakers and all the accoutrements one could possibly desire for that perfect cup of coffee.

3 Melissinos Art

Come here *(see p89)* for made-to-measure handcrafted leather sandals, inspired by ancient Greek designs – the perfect footwear for a summer on the beach. Melissinos' famous customers included The Beatles, Leonard Cohen and Kate Moss.

Baklava from Karavan

4 Karavan

MAP M2 ▪ Voukourestiou 11
▪ 210 364 1540

A tiny treasure trove of sweet treats, Karavan sells the best baklava and *kataïfi* (syrupy pastries made with shredded dough) in town.

Athens' Flea Market

5 Athens' Flea Market

If you have an eye for an authentic antique, you can pick up outstanding bargains at this sprawling and varied Sunday market *(see p87)*. Wake up early, though – there's not much point arriving here after 11am, as the streets become jam-packed and most of the treasures disappear quickly.

6 Elena Votsi

Elena Votsi's items are available in London, Paris and New York, but the full range can be viewed at her boutiques in Athens and Ydra island *(see p105)*. Votsi works mainly with gold, lapis lazuli, coral, amethyst and aquamarine, and her trade-marks are thick-set, rough-cut necklaces and knuckle-duster rings. Votsi is also known as the designer of the front of the 2004 Olympic summer games medal.

7 Korres
MAP D4 ■ Ermou 4, Syndagma

The humble origins of this natural-based, environmentally and animal-friendly cosmetics brand that has taken Europe and the United States by storm lie in this small homeopathic pharmacy. The full collection of haircare, suncare, and face and body lotions is available here. Delight the senses with refreshing citrus body spray, the sweetly spicy coriander shower gel or the orange blossom facial cleanser.

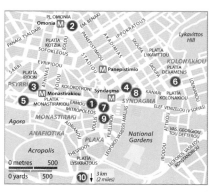

8 Zoumboulakis Gallery
MAP M3 ■ Kriezotou 6
■ www.zoumboulakis.gr

A veritable Athenian institution, this shop showcases contemporary art, furniture, ceramics and sculptures. Also, there is an excellent range of limited-edition prints and posters by established artists, and exhibitions are held by up-and-coming Greek artists. Signed and numbered silkscreens are reasonably priced.

9 Kori
Bringing a new quality and sophistication to the words souvenir shop, Kori (see p81) stocks an eclectic mix of accessories and ornaments crafted by some of Greece's brightest and best young artists, as well as replicas of museum pieces and traditional pottery, icons and statuettes.

10 Pantopolion
A treasure trove for gourmets, this store (see p81) stocks an assortment of quality Greek regional produce, including thyme honey from Tinos, mastiha liqueur from Hios, black olives from Kalamata, and dried herbs and teas from Mount Taygetos. Pantopolion is run by two retired lawyers, who also offer talks and organize tastings. They also package a selection of items in presentation boxes for you to take home.

Kori, a treasure trove of elegant Greek souvenirs

⭲🔟 Athens for Free

Buskers on Platía Monastirakiou

1 Street Performers
Pass by Platía Monastirakiou *(see p86)* at almost any time of day to be entertained by street artists, who perform everything from mime acts and fire-eating, to juggling and busking.

2 Acropolis for Free
There is free entry to the Acropolis *(see pp12–13)* on 6 Mar (in memory of Melina Mercouri), 18 Apr (International Monuments Day), 18 May (International Museums Day), 5 Jun (International Environment Day), the last weekend of Sep (European Heritage Day), 28 Oct (Ohi Day) and every first Sun of the month from 1 Nov to 31 Mar. The same applies to the National Archaeological Museum *(see pp20–21)*.

3 Benaki Museum for Free
The Benaki Museum *(see pp26–7)* in Kolonaki traces the development of Greek culture through the ages and offers free entry every Thursday, when it also has extended opening hours, 10am–midnight.

4 Byzantine Break
On the busy shopping street of Ermou, take a look inside tiny Kapnikarea *(see p87)*, a peaceful Byzantine church animated by flickering candles and bearded priests amid wafts of incense.

5 European Music Day
Each year on 21 June (the longest day of the year), free, open-air concerts take place throughout Greece, with the main stage in Athens on Platía Kotzia near Platía Omonia *(see p93)*. Past performers include Transglobal Underground and Scissor Sisters.

6 Seaside Stroll
From Neo Faliro metro station, you can walk all the way along the coast to Piraeus, passing the fishing boats in the harbour at Mikrolimano *(see p111)*, flashy yachts moored up in Zea Marina *(see p109)* and informal cafés with fine sea views along Akti Themistokleous *(see p110)*.

Moored fishing boats and yachts in Piraeus

7 Musical Enlightenment

You can discover more about the sound, appearance and history of traditional Greek musical instruments at the educational and amusing Museum of Greek Musical Instruments *(see p48 and p78)* in Plaka, which offers free entry throughout the year.

8 Performing Soldiers

Every Sunday at 11am, you can watch the *evzones* (soldiers) at the ceremonial Changing of the Guard next to the Tomb of the Unknown Soldier, in front of the Parliament *(see p101)*, on Platía Syndagmatos.

Changing of the Guard ceremony

9 Panoramic Views

For a total escape from the urban bustle, hike up a steep winding path to the top of Lykavittos Hill *(see p102)* to enjoy glorious panoramic views over the entire city, with the sea and mountains visible in the distance. Great photo opportunities – and a free workout, too.

10 Market Colours

The Central Market *(see p94)* offers an authentic Athenian shopping experience. You don't have to buy anything, but the stalls – piled high with seasonal fruit and vegetables, fresh seafood displayed on crushed ice and slightly gory meat products – make this a great venue for capturing local colour and atmosphere.

TOP 10 MONEY-SAVING TIPS

Travelling by ferry

1 Ferries going to the nearby islands, are slightly cheaper (although slower) than hydrofoils and catamarans.

2 When eating out, opt for *hyma* (bulk) wine, served by the carafe. It's cheap and cheerful, while bottled wine tends to be expensive.

3 Most the main attractions in central Athens are within walking distance of one another, so you rarely need to use public transport. Just be sure to wear comfortable shoes.

4 If you use public transport, be aware that a one-day travel ticket (valid for bus, tram and metro) costs €4.50; a five-day ticket €9. EU citizens over 65s, and under 18s, with ID cards receive a 50 per cent discount.

5 *Souvlaki* (kebab in pita bread) makes a tasty, nutritious takeaway meal, and is a cheap alternative to a sit-down lunch.

6 Online private rental sites such as Airbnb offer comfortable and often central accommodation in privately owned apartments, which are generally cheaper than hotels.

7 Tap water in Athens is perfectly good to drink, so you don't have to buy bottled water. Bring a canteen instead.

8 The *enieo* (joint) Acropolis ticket (valid three days) gives you access to 10 other ancient sites, so be sure to keep it safe to avoid paying twice.

9 The National Archaeological Museum *enieo* gives you access to the Byzantine and Christian Museum, the Numismatic Museum and the Epigraphical Museum.

10 At the beach, you have to pay for a sun bed or umbrella, so take a towel and straw mat and lie on the sand.

🔟 Festivals and Events

1 Epiphany
6 Jan
The "Blessing of the Waters", when young men dive for crosses cast into the water by priests at ports and beaches; it's a year's good luck for the successful divers.

2 Apokries
Feb–Mar
The Greek Orthodox Carnival begins 56 days before Easter Sunday. Festivities, especially glamorous masquerade parties, last for days. In Athens, the colourful celebrations centre on Plaka, where the streets are packed with revellers and masked musicians.

Flying kites on Clean Monday

3 Clean Monday
First day of Lent (Feb/Mar)
Greeks celebrate this day, which is also the Carnival's end by going to the country and flying kites; in Athens, the sky above Philopappos Hill is usually filled with them.

4 National Day/ Annunciation
25 Mar
Military parades with tanks, guns and battalions celebrate the start of the Greek independence revolt against the Ottomans in 1821. Annunciation to the Mother of God is also observed, linking religion and nationalism.

Eggs dyed red for Easter

5 Easter
Apr
This is the most important event on the Orthodox calendar, far outweighing Christmas. Highlights of the Holy Week include – Thursday evening Crucifixion liturgy; Friday processions by parishes parading flower-covered biers of Christ in effigy; the midnight Resurrection Mass on Saturday – concluding in fireworks (and, in remote villages, gunfire or tossed dynamite). On Sunday, families enjoy a meal of roast lamb, with eggs dyed red (symbolizing both the blood and rebirth of Christ).

6 Athens/Epidauros (Epidaurus) Festival
Jun–Sep ▪ www.greekfestival.gr
Ancient Greeks performed timeless tragedies in the Odeon of Herodes Atticus and the theatres of Epidauros. Following this ancient tradition, every summer, the world's greatest singers, dancers and actors perform under moonlight at these venues. The festival has hosted the performances of Harlem Gospel Choir, Gérard Depardieu and Isabella Rossellini.

Performance at the Epidauros festival

Rockwave (Jul)
Jul ■ www.rockwavefestival.gr

This three-day festival, at the Terra Vibe open-air venue, is Greece's hottest music ticket of the year. The line-up includes huge Greek and international pop, rock and alternative acts.

 Feast of the Dormition
15 Aug

Absolutely everything in town closes for the Dormition of the Mother of God, which is second only to Easter in the Orthodox calendar. Many "Marias" celebrate their name-day today (otherwise on 8 September or 21 November).

9 Ohi Day
28 Oct

A national holiday, Ohi Day celebrates Greece's rejection of Mussolini's ultimatum during World War II. A big military parade, culminating at Platía Syndagma, is staged in Athens.

Athens Marathon

10 Athens Marathon
Early Nov

Athletes from around the world retrace the course of Pheidippides, antiquity's most celebrated runner. In 490 BC, the Greeks defeated the Persians at Marathon in a historic battle for independence (see p130). Pheidippides ran the 42 km (26 miles) to Athens, announced the outcome ("Victory!"), then died of exhaustion. Today's runners have the advantage of water stops, a cooler climate and cheering crowds en route from Marathonas to the Kallimarmaro Stadium (see p101) to ease the arduous feat.

TOP 10 SAINTS' DAYS

St Nicholas Day celebrations

1 Agios Vasilios/St Basil (1 Jan)
Families eat *Vasilopita* (Basil's cake), into which a coin has been baked. Finding the coin brings a year's good luck.

2 O Prodromos/St John the Baptist (7 Jan)
The day John baptised Christ in the Jordan river.

3 St Athanasios (18 Jan)
The church auctions off donated gifts in honour of Athanasios of Alexandria, one of Orthodoxy's three holy Fathers.

4 Agia Philothei (19 Feb)
Athens' patron saint, this 16th-century abbess was martyred for refusing to let Muslims seize her nuns for harem duties.

5 Agios Georgios/St George (23 Apr)
The dragon-slayer is the patron of the military and shephards.

6 Agia Irini/St Irene (5 May)
Born a 4th-century Persian princess, Irini became a zelous Christian. She is the patroness of the national police force.

7 Agios Dimitrios/St Demetrios (26 Oct)
The greatest celebrations are in Thessaloniki, where this martyr, whose wounds ran with myrrh instead of blood, is patron saint.

8 St Catherine (25 Nov)
This famous Alexandrian martyr is honoured as the protectress of infants, maidens and female students.

9 St Stylianos (26 Nov)
Shown holding a swaddled infant, this is the patron of young children. He protects the unborn, and cures barrenness.

10 Agios Nikolaos/St Nicholas (6 Dec)
Celebrations honouring the patron saint of sailors are especially festive in coastal suburbs and on islands.

Athens Area by Area

The 4th-century BC theatre at Delphi

🔟 Plaka, Makrygianni and Koukaki

The winding alleyways of Plaka, the old quarter below the Acropolis, are easily the most charming part of Athens. Naturally, they are also the most visited, and in midsummer some streets can be packed with touts and cheap gift stalls. But Plaka also conceals places of untouched delight. The formerly working-class areas of Makrygianni and Koukaki have shaken off old dust, and must-see museums, fine-dining restaurants and ultra-hip clubs are the new order of the day.

Relief sculpture on the Roman era, Tower of the Winds

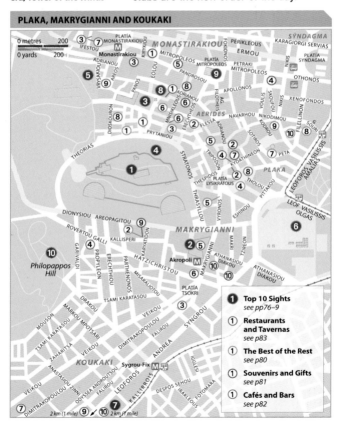

PLAKA, MAKRYGIANNI AND KOUKAKI

	Top 10 Sights see pp76–9
①	Restaurants and Tavernas see p83
①	The Best of the Rest see p80
①	Souvenirs and Gifts see p81
①	Cafés and Bars see p82

The impressive Acropolis, dominating the Plaka skyline

1 Acropolis

The sacred rock of the Acropolis (see pp12–13) dominates Plaka, and its different temples are clearly visible from all angles throughout the neighbourhood. Legend holds that it was on this rock that Athena (see p53) won dominion of Athens from Poseidon, and it has been devoted to worshipping the goddess since 650 BC.

2 Acropolis Museum

Designed by internationally renowned architect Bernard Tschumi, this all-glass $100 million museum (see p13) opened in mid-2008. It was built with the intention to provide a fitting home to Greece's greatest treasures: the marble sculptures and architectural features of the frieze which once adorned the Parthenon. Only half of the frieze remains in Greece (see pp14–15).

Statue, Acropolis Museum

3 Roman Forum and Tower of the Winds

The Athenians, under Roman governor Nikias, built this Roman marketplace (see pp24–5), which replaced the original Greek Agora, and the townspeople and Nikias are commemorated on the Gate of Athena Archegetis. Its most striking feature, the Tower of the Winds, was built around 50 BC, during the rule of Julius Caesar. There was no other building like it in the ancient world: eight-sided, each side sculpted with a personification of the wind from that direction: Boreas, Kaikias, Apeliotes, Euros, Notos, Lips, Zephyros and Skiron.

4 Anafiotika

Clinging to the side of the Acropolis is Athens' loveliest and quirkiest neighbourhood. It was built during the 1830s by craftsmen from the Cycladic island of Anafi, brought to Athens after the War of Independence to build King Otto's palace. They re-created a pocket of home here, all island-style, blue-and-white houses, covered with banks of bougainvillea, in a maze of tiny passageways. Many descendants of the original Anafi workers still live here.

Peaceful courtyard in Anafiotika

Exhibit at Museum of Greek Folk Art

5 Museum of Greek Folk Art

MAP J3 ■ www.melt.gr

This museum (see p49) has a vast collection of rich, beautiful folk art, from jewellery to decorate and cover the entire body to fine embroideries worked with gold and silver thread. Also included are traditional tapestries and shadow puppets. The museum will reopen in 2021 in a new location in Monastiraki.

6 Temple of Olympian Zeus

All that remains of Greece's largest temple, a shrine to Zeus, is 16 columns. But, as they stand alone, silhouetted by the bright Attic sky, their majesty still overwhelms. Inside the temple was a colossal gold-and-ivory sculpture of the god, a copy of the original at Olympia, one of the Seven Wonders of the ancient world (see pp36–7).

7 National Museum of Contemporary Art

MAP C6 ■ Kallirois & Frantzi, Makrygianni ■ 211 101 9000 ■ Adm ■ www.emst.gr

The long-awaited National Museum of Contemporary Art (EMST) opened in 2017 in the Fix building, a former brewery dating from 1957. Their permanent collection is small, but it is always worth calling in for the interesting temporary exhibits.

8 Museum of Greek Popular Musical Instruments

MAP K4 ■ Diogenous 1–3 ■ 210 215 0198 ■ Open 10am–2pm Thu–Tue, 2–6pm Wed

At this unassuming museum (see p54), you can see and hear the Middle Eastern and European influences on Greek music, and how Greeks transformed them into something of their own. The instruments themselves are beautiful, often intricately inlaid with silver, ivory and tortoiseshell. There are plans to move the museum to make it a part of the Museum of Greek Folk Art.

Temple of Olympian Zeus

Entrance to Mitropoli

9 Mitropoli
MAP K3 ■ Platía Mitropoleos
■ Open 6:30am–8pm daily

Lavishly appointed, Athens Cathedral is one of the city's best-known landmarks (see p47). The archbishop of Greece (once the nation's most influential person) gives addresses here, and it is regularly packed for Athens' high-society weddings. Of greater artistic importance, though, is tiny Panagia Gorgoepikoös ("little Mitropoli"), next door. This 12th- century church incorporates Hellenistic, Roman and Byzantine masonry, depicting ancient feasts.

Monument at Philopappos Hill

10 Philopappos Hill
Next to the Acropolis rock, pine-and-cypress-clad Philopappos Hill (see pp34–5) offers a cool, green place to stroll. The peak, marked by the tomb and monument of Roman-Syrian prince Gaius Julius Antiochos Philopappos, offers sweeping views from the Acropolis to the sea. In summer, the Dora Stratou Dance Troupe puts on regular performances of Greek folk dances in a theatre nestled among the pines.

A MORNING IN PLAKA

▶ EARLY MORNING

Hike up to the **Acropolis** (see p77) early, to beat the heat and the worst of the crowds. Spend an hour or so admiring the temples.

Come down from the Acropolis and turn left onto the **Dionysiou Areopagitou** walkway (see p60). Your Acropolis ticket gives you free entry into the **Theatre of Dionysos** (see p13), where many great classical dramas were first staged.

Head back out to the walkway to visit the **Acropolis Museum** (see p77). Next, head to **Platía Lysikratous**, named after the unusual monument to the winner of a 335 BC choral competition. Stop for a frappé in one of the leafy cafés nearby.

LATE MORNING

From the square, head up to the charming 19th-century quarter of **Anafiotika** (see p77) to explore its twisting alleys.

Leave by Prytaniou, stopping in the quiet garden of the Byzantine **Church of the Holy Sepulchre** (see p80), and lighting a candle from its famed holy flame.

From Prytaniou, turn right on Mnisikleous and left on Kyrristou for a choice of either the **Museum of Greek Musical Instruments**, while it is still at this location, or the **Roman Forum and Tower of the Winds** (see p77). Finally, head back a block to **O Platanos** (see p83), for a hefty Greek lunch under a huge plane tree.

See map on p76 ←

The Best of the Rest

1 Kanellopoulos Museum
MAP J4 ▪ Theorias 12 ▪ 210 321
2313 ▪ 8am–3pm Tue–Sun ▪ Adm

A miscellany of privately-collected
high-quality antiquities on display
in a Neo-Classical mansion.

2 Lalaounis Museum
MAP J5 ▪ Kallisperi 12 &
Karyatidon ▪ 210 922 1044 ▪ 9am–3pm
Tue–Sat (until 9pm Wed), 11am–4pm
Sun ▪ Adm (free Sat)

Jeweller Ilias Lalaounis showcases
his creations at this museum.

Jewellery at Lalaounis Museum

3 Church of the Holy Sepulchre
MAP K4 ▪ Between Prytaniou and
Erotokritou

Miracles are associated with this
beautiful 18th-century church, and
many flock here at Easter to light
candles from the holy flame, which
comes directly from the Holy
Sepulchre in Jerusalem.

4 Church of Agia Ekaterini
MAP L5 ▪ Off Platia Lysikratous

The columns of an ancient temple
still stand beneath the courtyard
of this lovely Byzantine church.

5 Choregic Monument of Lysikrates
MAP L5 ▪ Platia Lysikratous

Built in 335 BC, this monument
honours Lysikrates, sponsor of the
Dionysian Choral competition (see p42).

6 The Bath House of the Winds
MAP K4 ▪ Kyrristou 8 ▪ 210 324 5957
▪ 8am–3pm Mon, Wed–Sun ▪ Adm

A refurbished Ottoman bath-house
from the 16th century, this small
museum places public baths in their
social context.

7 Frissiras Museum of Contemporary European Painting
MAP L4 ▪ Monis Asteriou 3 & 7
▪ 210 323 4678 ▪ 11am–6pm Wed–
Fri, 11am–5pm Sat & Sun ▪ Adm
▪ www.frissirasmuseum.com

A museum of over 3,000 works of top
post-war Greek and European artists.

8 Agia Triada
MAP L4 ▪ Filellinon

The largest medieval church in the
city dates originally from 1031 and is
now Athens' Russian Orthodox church.

9 Museum of Greek Children's Art
MAP L4 ▪ Kodrou 9 ▪ 210 331 2621
▪ Sep–Jul: 10am–2pm Tue–Sat,
11am–2pm Sun ▪ Closed Aug ▪ Adm

Admire works by young artists living
in mountain tribes, cities and refugee
centres. Many activities for kids.

10 Jewish Museum
MAP L4 ▪ Nikis 39
▪ 210 322 5582 ▪ 9am–2:30pm
Mon–Fri, 10am–2pm Sun ▪ Adm
▪ www.jewishmuseum.gr

The collection's 15,000 items tell the
story of the Jews in Greece.

Exhibit at the Jewish Museum

Souvenirs and Gifts

Arts and crafts objects for sale at Forget Me Not

1 Pantopolion
MAP M3 ■ Dimitrakopoulou 34
This is the place *(see p69)* to purchase traditional Greek foodstuffs made by monks at Makariotissa Monastery in Viotia, plus a vast selection of Greek wines and local craft beers.

2 Ioanna Kourbela
MAP C4 ■ Adrianou 109
■ ionnakourela.com
Youthful, flowing clothes made from natural organic fabrics such as cotton, linen, wool and silk.

3 Pagani
MAP C4 ■ Pandrosou 59
■ www.pagani.gr
This handmade decorative arts shop features crafts and jewellery reflecting Greek tradition and culture.

4 Kori
MAP K3 ■ Mitropoleos 13
& Voulis ■ www.kori.gr
This little shop sells signed and numbered artworks by some of the country's latest talents.

5 The Athens Gallery
MAP C4 ■ Pandrosou 14
■ www.athensgallery.gr
This gallery represents both Greek and foreign artists. All the sculptures and fine art pieces explore Greek lifestyle and culture.

6 Forget Me Not
MAP C4 ■ Adrianou 100
■ www.forgetmenotathens.gr
This gift shop offers unusual items by contemporary Greek designers, including T-shirts, ceramics and jewellery.

7 O Brettos
MAP L4 ■ Kydathineon 41
Pop in for a bottle of this distillery's *(see p82)* barrelled ouzo or wine, and finish with a shot of surprisingly sweet *mastiha* (liqeur made with mastic). Admire the barrels under the eaves.

8 Olive Tree Store
MAP C4 ■ Adrianou 67
This family-run store stocks bowls, spoons and chopping boards made from olive wood. They also arrange shipping.

9 Lalaounis Museum Jewellery Shop
MAP J5 ■ Corner of Karyatidon & Kallisperi 12
Some of the world's most glamorous gold creations are to be found at Ilias Lalounis' celebrated jewellery house.

10 ArtShot
MAP K6 ■ Lembesi 11 ■ www.sophiagaitani.gr
This shop on arty Lembesi street offers jewellery, clothing and accessories by Greek artists.

See map on p76

Cafés and Bars

1 Klepsydra
MAP K4 ■ Thrasyvoulou 9
This tiny, quiet bar-café located beyond the Tower of the Winds is surrounded by flower pots and pastel-hued buildings.

2 Melina
MAP K4 ■ Lysiou 22, Aerides
This pink-and-gilt shrine to the late Greek actress and national heroine Melina Mercouri was once her favourite café.

3 Couleur Locale
MAP J3 ■ Normanou 3
This rooftop bar serves excellent coffee and other drinks, and offers one of the most stunning views of the Acropolis in Plaka.

4 O Brettos
MAP L4 ■ Kydathineon 41
The walls here are lined with bottles of home-made, brilliantly coloured liquors that glow like stained-glass windows. The drinks are good, too.

5 Acropolis Museum Café
MAP C5 ■ Dionysiou Areopagitou 15
Located on the museum's ground floor, this café-restaurant serves coffee, drinks and light snacks on a terrace overlooking the excavations found under the museum. There is free admission at the ticket desk for those coming just for the café.

6 Yiasemi, Plaka
MAP K4 ■ Mnisikleous 23
With tables on the stone steps below the Acropolis, this café-bistrot also serves vegetarian buffet breakfasts. There's a fireplace indoors in winter.

7 TAF-The Art Foundation
MAP B4 ■ Normanou 5
This multi-purpose art and culture space is housed in a beautiful 19th-century building, and has a convivial bar-café located in the inner courtyard. It can be hard to find: look for the small wooden door.

8 7 Food Sins
MAP L4 ■ Platía Filomousou Eterias 1, Plaka
A gastro pub where creative cuisine is on equal footing with the pricy drinks menu.

9 Vryssaki
MAP J3 ■ Vrysakiou 17, Plaka
An arts venue and bar, with rooftop terrace overlooking the ancient Agora, Vryssaki encourages all sorts of experimental activities.

10 Hitchcocktales
MAP K6 ■ Porinou 10, Makrygianni
Set in a refurbished industrial space, this place is open only at night. It serves food and drinks with menu names inspired by Alfred Hitchcock's films.

Interiors of the Acropolis Museum Café

Restaurants and Tavernas

1 O Platanos
MAP K4 ▪ Diogenous 4
▪ 210 322 0666 ▪ Closed Sun
▪ No credit cards ▪ €

Eat grilled or oven-baked meat accompanied by *horta* (amranth greens), washed down with some of the best *retsina (see p65)* in Attica.

Cod dish at Bakaliarakia tou Damigou

2 Bakaliarakia tou Damigou
MAP L4 ▪ Kydathineon 41 (basement)
▪ 210 322 5084 ▪ Closed Mon ▪ No credit cards ▪ €

This family run local favourite has been serving up fried cod with garlic sauce since 1865.

3 Mani Mani
MAP C6 ▪ Falirou 10 ▪ 210 921 8180 ▪ €€

A spiral staircase leads to modern dining rooms with just a hint of rustic style. On the menu is nouvelle mainland cuisine.

4 Strofi
MAP B5 ▪ Rovertou Galli 25
▪ 210 921 4130 ▪ €€

Offers great rooftop views and food that is a cut above the typical taverna fare. Audience and performers from the Herodes Atticus often come here.

5 To Kafenion
MAP K4 ▪ Epiharmou 1 & Tripodon ▪ 210 324 6916 ▪ €

Located on a side street, this is often missed by tourists. Regional dishes are lifted with home-made sauces.

PRICE CATEGORIES
For a three-course meal for one with half a bottle of wine (or equivalent meal), taxes and extra charges.

€ under €40   €€ €40–€60   €€€ over €60

---

6 To Kati Allo
MAP K6 ▪ Hatzichristou 12
▪ 210 922 3071 ▪ €

On the street flanking the Acropolis Museum to the south, this tavern offers delicious Greek comfort food.

7 Garyfallo Kanela
MAP B6 ▪ Odyssea Androutsou 35, Koukaki ▪ 210 924 5332 ▪ Closed Sun & Mon D ▪ €

Homestyle, aromatic casserole dishes with options for vegetarians. They serve three kinds of *hyma* wine *(see p65)*.

8 Dioskouroi
MAP J4 ▪ Dioskouron 13, Plaka ▪ €

At the tourist heart of Athens, this café-taverna draws locals, especially young ones, who come for the platters *pikilia* (medley of small snacks).

Pikilia **at Dioskouroi**

9 Fabrika of Euphrosinos
MAP B6 ▪ Anastasiou Zinni 34
▪ 210 924 6354 ▪ €€

Enjoy authentic Greek cuisine and don't miss out on the desserts. They offer vegetarian food and boast an excellent wine list.

10 Hytra
MAP T2 ▪ 107–109 Syngrou Avenue ▪ 217 707 1118 ▪ €€€

Located close to the new opera house this restaurant *(see p67)* offers a modern take on traditional Greek dishes.

See map on p76

TOP10 Monastiraki, Psyrri, Gazi and Thisio

For decades these old neighbourhoods of warehouses and workshops lay quiet, crumbling and neglected, enlivened only by the Monastiraki flea market, which spills out antiques, kitsch and junk from Platía Avissynias. However, the appeal of a central location and some 21st-century ingenuity combined to create an authentically funky atmosphere. This part of the city is a hub for hipster clubs, cafés and restaurants. Gentrification hasn't robbed these districts of their character, though. Rather, craftsmen's shops and industrial buildings nestle side-by-side with edgy clubs, hole-in-the-wall Greek music dives and squares filled with outdoor cafés and bars. Adding to the mix are views of marble antiquities at the Agora and Kerameikos, Athens' greenest archaeological sites.

An exhibit at Technopolis

1 Athinais
MAP A3 ▪ Kastorias 34–6, Votanikos ▪ 210 348 0000 ▪ www.athinais.com.gr ▪ Museum: open 9am–10pm daily

Formerly a silk factory, Athinais is now a trendy, upmarket arts centre. It houses a stylish resto-bar, a music hall, a theatre and an art museum with permanent and temporary exhibits.

2 Hadrian's Library
MAP J3 ▪ Open 8am–3pm daily ▪ Adm ▪ www.odysseus.culture.gr

Roman Emperor Hadrian built this sumptuous "library" (really more of

Hadrian's Library

a luxurious forum) in AD 132 (see p44). It featured a marble courtyard, mosaic floors, concert areas and a small area for storing library scrolls, all surrounded by exquisite Corinthian columns.

Technopolis
MAP A4 ■ Pireos 100
■ 210 346 1589

Dating from 1862, this enormous complex is housed in a former gasworks which functioned until 1984, giving the area its name (Gazi). In 1999 it was converted into a huge arts centre, hosting top-notch exhibitions, concerts and arts spaces. The creation of Technopolis revitalized the entire area, making Gazi one of the liveliest nightlife hubs of the city.

Kerameikos
A green oasis in the middle of factories and transportation depots, this is the site of the oldest and largest burial ground in Attica

Kerameikos burial ground

(see pp30–31). There are walls and gates of the ancient city, and running through the site is the Sacred Way. Outside the site, the road continues – still incongruously named Sacred Way despite its congested traffic and often empty warehouses.

MONASTIRAKI, PSYRRI, GAZI AND THISIO

⑤ Platía Monastirakiou
MAP J3

There has been a church and monastery on this site since at least the 10th century. After most of the monastic buildings were lost during 19th-century excavations, the area was renamed Monastiraki – "little monastery". Built in 1678, the Pantánassa church, is dedicated to the Dormition of the Mother of God.

Platía Monastirakiou

⑥ Benaki Pireos Annexe
MAP A4 ■ Pireos 138
■ www.benaki.gr ■ Adm

In a renovated 1960s Lada car showroom, this modern exhibition space stages temporary art shows, with an emphasis on contemporary photography, painting, sculpture, installations and architecture. Similar to the main Benaki museum, there is an excellent gift shop and small bistro-café. The building envelopes a central courtyard, which is used for open-air summer performances.

THE JEWISH COMMUNITY

The area of Psyrri and Kerameikos has been heavily settled by Greek Jews since the 3rd century BC. In 1944, the Nazis occupying Athens sent more than half the population to concentration camps; however, the community has slowly recovered to about 3000, and has become a centre of Greek Jewish life.

⑦ Platía Agias Irinis
MAP K3 ■ Eolou St & Skouze

This popular square has lived many lives, from being a 19th-century business district to a flower market and even a garment district. Neglected for a few decades, it regained its splendour and found a new identity during the 2000s, owing to Eolou's pedestrianisation, as a hotspot for trendy yet traditional eateries, stylish bars and cafés located around the butter-coloured Agia Irini church, dating from 1850s.

⑧ Agora and Agora Museum

One of the most interesting archaeological sites in Greece, the Agora (see pp16–19) is where Socrates "corrupted" youth, St Paul preached and converted his first followers, and the first decisions in the fledgling Athenian democracy were made. Don't miss the wonderfully preserved Temple of Hephaistos, or the recreated Stoa of Attalos, now home to the excellent Agora Museum.

Covered walkway of the Stoa of Attalos, which houses the Agora Museum

9 Kapnikarea

MAP K3 ■ Kapnikarea & Ermou
■ 8am–2pm daily

One of Athens' greatest pleasures is walking down a crowded street and suddenly finding yourself face-to-face with a tiny, centuries-old monument in the midst of all the modernity. The beautiful 11th-century church known as Kapnikarea, smack in the middle of the shopping street of Ermou and beautifully decorated with frescoes by master Photis Kontoglou in the 1950s, provides just such a moment. Possibly built over the ruins of an ancient shrine to a goddess, the church is appropriately dedicated to the Presentation of the Mother of God.

Photis Kontoglou frescoes, Kapnikarea

10 Athens' Flea Market

MAP J3 ■ Platía Avissynias & Ifestou

Platía Avissynias comes alive on Sunday mornings, when Athens' biggest and most colourful flea market fills the space and spills out to the streets around it. Here's where you'll find a little bit of everything: pink cut-glass Turkish liqueur sets, old and ornate phones that still work, beautiful antique carved-wood desks, and piles of fantastic kitsch and junk. Use your haggling skills. Shops in Ifestou, which is close by, are open daily.

SUNDAY MARKETS

▶ MORNING

Start the day at **Telaro** (Éolou 33 • 210 32 43 840) diagonally opposite Agia Irini church and marvel at the chanting after 9:30am.

Next, head for Psyrri to **Melissinos Art** (see p89). Owner Stavros is no longer here, but his son Pandelis will custom-fit you a classic pair of Greek sandals.

Proceed to the historic church at the centre of **Platía Monastirakiou**, and then take a coffee break at **360 Cocktail Bar** (see p61) and enjoy the lovely Acropolis views. Next, stroll towards the ancient halls and courtyard of **Hadrian's Library** (see pp84–5).

EARLY AFTERNOON

Head over to the **Agora**, the sprawling marketplace that was Athens' heart for centuries. Make sure not to miss the wonderfully well-preserved **Temple of Hephaistos** (see p14) and the restored Stoa of Attalos, home to the excellent **Agora Museum**.

After you're warmed up, cross over the metro tracks to **Ifestou** for the fun of haggling at the lively **Athens' Flea Market** at Platía Avissynias. It's hard to resist buying at least something, though by this stage of the day it is more likely to be kitschy junk than bargain antiques.

Once you're done, retire with your booty to **Oineas** (p90) to enjoy a long lunch, while the marketplace closes down and the music and drinking start up.

See map on pp84–5 ←

The Best of the Rest

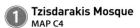
Flea market in front of Tzisdarakis Mosque

1 Tzisdarakis Mosque
MAP C4

With a brightly painted mihrab, this 18th-century mosque houses specialist ceramics. It is undergoing restoration, so check before visiting.

2 Museum of Greek Gastronomy
MAP C3 ▪ Agiou Dimitriou 13
▪ www.gastronomymuseum.gr

A museum dedicated to Greek cuisine, with temporary exhibitions focusing on particular periods or regions. They also run workshops and classes.

3 Bernier/Eliades Gallery
MAP A4 ▪ Eptahalkou 11
▪ www.bernier-eliades.gr

This premiere gallery exhibits local as well as international artists.

4 Cine Psiri
MAP B3 ▪ Sarri 40–44
▪ 210 324 7234

This great outdoor cinema frequently shows black-and-white classics and foreign films (subtitled in Greek) during the summer months.

5 Beth Shalom Synagogue
MAP B4 ▪ Melidoni 5

Originally Sephardic, this is Athens' main synagogue. Before World War II, this area was the centre of the city's Jewish community. There is an older and smaller synagogue at Melidoni 8.

6 Athenaeum
MAP B4 ▪ Adrianou 3
▪ www.athenaeum.com.gr

This conservatory, created shortly before the death of world-famous soprano Maria Callas, hosts annual Grand Prix contests.

7 Adrianou
MAP K3

The stretch of this street from the Thisio metro station to Hadrian's Library has wonderful views of the Agora and the Acropolis.

8 Herakleidon Museum
MAP A4 ▪ Iraklidon 16 & Apostolou Pavlou 37 ▪ 9am–5pm Mon–Fri ▪ www.herakleidon-art.gr

Offering exceptional gift items, this private museum also has permanent as well as temporary exhibits.

Exhibition at Herakleidon Museum

9 Benaki Museum of Islamic Art
MAP B3 ▪ Agion Asomaton 22 & Dipylou ▪ 210 325 1311
▪ www.benaki.gr

In a Neo-Classical town house, four large exhibition rooms display Islamic ceramics, woodcarvings, metalwork, glassware and textiles.

10 Odos Iraklidon
MAP A4

Lined with cafés and bars, this crowded street feels both old world and fresh, and bustles day and night.

Bargains, Antiques and Market Stalls

1 Bahar
MAP K2 ■ Evripidou 31–33

The whole area around the central meat market teems with old, family-run shops selling traditional foodstuffs. Bahar is one of the best-known for herbs and spices.

2 Artemis
MAP B4 ■ Thisiou 10

You never know what you might unearth among the books, coins, stamps, jewellery and antiques in this potential treasure trove.

3 Athens' Flea Market
Everything under the sun, from ancient coins to fake designer sunglasses, frilly knickers and genuine antiques at rock-bottom prices (see p87).

Striking antiques at Martinos

4 D. Gounaris
MAP J3 ■ Ifaistou 11

A tiny alcove manages to stock a fine selection of traditional wooden *tavli* (backgammon) boards as well as chess sets. Prices from as low as €10.

5 Sigma-Stoupakis
MAP J3 ■ Ermou 86

Purveyor of handmade wooden furniture and home accessories in styles that range from contemporary to retro.

6 Melissinos Art
MAP J3 ■ Ag. Theklas 2
■ www.melissinospoet sandalmaker.com

"Poet sandal-maker" Stavros Melissinos took over his father's shop for handmade leather sandals in 1954, which has drawn a lot of celebrity clientele. The shop is still a favourite, with over 30 basic styles of sandals.

7 Martinos Antiques
MAP K3 ■ Pandrosou 50
■ www.martinosart.gr

Three-floor shop offering furniture, gold and silver, paintings, carpets and books from all over the world.

8 Centre of Hellenic Tradition
MAP K3 ■ Mitropoleos 59
■ www.kelp.gr

A warehouse of Greek handicrafts. If you only have time for one souvenir stop, make this it.

9 Aristokratikon
MAP L3
■ Karageorgi Servias 9

Made from the finest Greek ingredients, these chocolates are strictly for connoisseurs.

10 Kalyviotis
MAP L3 ■ Ermou 8

Thread and fabric, bead- and button-filled shops populate the area around Ermou and Perikleous. Kalyviotis is the best one-stop haberdashery.

Sandals from Melissinos Art

See map on pp84–5 ←

Places to Eat

PRICE CATEGORIES

For a three-course meal for one with half a bottle of wine (or equivalent meal), taxes and extra charges.

€ under €40   €€ €40–€60   €€€ over €60

1 Funky Gourmet
MAP A3 ▪ Paramythias 13 & Salaminos, Keramikos-Metaxourgio ▪ 210 524 2727 ▪ €€€

Quirky spot with a minimalist-chic upper-floor dining room, creating beautiful dishes from local produce.

Traditional interior of Oineas

2 Oineas
MAP J2 ▪ Esopou 9, Psyrri ▪ 210 321 5614 ▪ €

High-quality, modern taverna food with a twist. Share a massive house salad, then try the stuffed lamb, or the orzo hotpot with crayfish.

3 Thanassis
MAP K3
▪ Mitropoleos 67
▪ 210 324 4705 ▪ €

Athens' most famous *souvlaki* and beef kebab joint has been serving up sliced meat, with cool *tzatziki*, wrapped in pittas, since the 19th century.

4 Mama Roux
MAP K2 ▪ Eolou 48
▪ 213 004 8382 ▪ €

A plate of *Souvlaki*

All-day gastropub with tall windows and a menu inspired by European, American and Asian food.

5 Butcher Shop
MAP A4 ▪ Persefonis 19, Gazi
▪ 210 341 3440 ▪ €

The butcher's-style interior includes a window display hung with sausages. Meat dishes are supplemented by generous portions of vegetables. Try the seafood here and do not miss out on the desserts.

6 Ta Karamanlidika Tou Fani
MAP J2 ▪ Sokratous 1 & Evripidou, Psyrri ▪ 210 325 4184 ▪ €

With in a renovated Neo-Classical interior, this deli-*mezedopolio* serves inner-Anatolian (Karamanian) influenced recipes such as pickled okra and 'finger' kebab in yogurt sauce.

7 Aleria
MAP A3 ▪ Megalou Alexandrou 57, Metaxourgio ▪ 210 522 2633 ▪ €€€

Come here for crab with fennel and kohlrabi, sweetbreads with fricassee, or a choice of tasting menus. The dining room opens on to a courtyard.

8 Athiri
MAP A3 ▪ Plateon 15
▪ 210 346 2983 ▪ €€€

Relaxed yet refined. Creative dishes include tuna *tataki* (yellow-fin tuna lightly singed in soy sauce), or the Iberico pork shoulder with giant Prespa beans and herbs.

9 Manas Kouzina Kouzina
MAP K3 ▪ Eolou 27
▪ 210 325 2335 ▪ €

Set in historic Agia Irini (see p66) square, this place offers changing menus.

10 Nikitas
MAP J2 ▪ Agion Anargyron 19, Psyrri
▪ 210 325 2591 ▪ €

Founded in 1967, this is probably the oldest taverna in Psyrri. The menu includes delicious grills, and boasts an excellent beer and wine selection.

Nightspots

Live music at Six D.O.G.S

1 Six D.O.G.S
MAP C4 ■ Avramiotou 68
■ www.sixdogs.gr

This cultural centre in the heart of Monastiraki focuses on visual art projects but also hosts workshops, live gigs, parties and film screenings.

2 Kapnikarea
MAP A4 ■ Hristopoulou 2, corner Ermou, Monastiraki

With a resonably priced menu, this *mezedopolio* is a perfect nightspot. It hosts live, acoustic rembetika sessions and is most lively during weekends.

3 Noel
MAP K2 ■ Kolokotroni 59B, Monastiraki

Set in the historic Kourtaki arcade, this bistro-bar has a quirky decor. It is famous for its fine cocktail menu.

4 Baba au Rum
MAP C4 ■ Klitiou 6

Sip exotic cocktails prepared with premium spirits, fresh juices and homemade syrups and liqueurs.

5 Hoxton
MAP A3 ■ Voutadon 42, Gazi

Located opposite Kerameikos metro station, this hip industrial-style lounge holds art and photography exhibitions.

6 A for Athens
MAP J3 ■ Miaouli 2–4

This sleekly designed rooftop bar offers views of Plaka and the Acropolis. Come for breakfast or an evening cocktail.

7 Underdog
MAP A4 ■ Iraklidon 8

In a beautiful Neo-Classical building, Underdog serves speciality coffees, cocktails, local and international craft beer, plus brunch every day from 10am.

8 Bios
MAP B3 ■ Pireos 84, Gazi

With a ground level bar and a basement club, Bios stages alternative theatre and concerts. A café on the first floor is open all day, or enjoy your drink in the open-air rooftop bar with a view of the Acropolis (Jun–Sep).

9 Faust
MAP K3 ■ Kalamiotou 11

Faust, with its black-and-red gothic style interior, is a venue for local theatre and live bands, and is also home to a lively bar and club. Music performances range from rock to jazz. Dancing takes over after 1am.

Trendy Booze Cooperativa

10 Booze Cooperativa
MAP C4 ■ Kolokotroni 57

An arty club with exhibitions, videos and alternative theatre. Downstairs are magazines and board games; upstairs is loud rock music.

See map on pp84–5

 Omonia and Exárhia

Exárhia and Omonia are among Athens' oldest, most well-worn districts. Though neither qualifies as beautiful, both are steeped in history, some of it quite recent. In 1973, the Polytechnic student uprising in Exárhia was crushed by the junta, but it did eventually lead to the fall of the military dictatorship. The students left behind an area full of tavernas, cafés and bars; this is also the best place to hear rembetika, the gritty Greek blues. Below Exárhia is seedy, clamorous Omonia, and just beyond is the colourful marketplace district.

Black-figure wine jug with a libation scene

1 Municipal Art Gallery
MAP B3 ■ Myllerou 32 & Leonidou ■ Open 10am–2pm & 5–9pm Tue–Sat, 10am–2pm Sun

All of the best-known modern Greek artists are represented here, in addition to works by 19th-century Saxon architect Ernst Ziller. On display are his plans for the Neo-Classical National Theatre and for the city's grandest private homes, now mostly converted to museums.

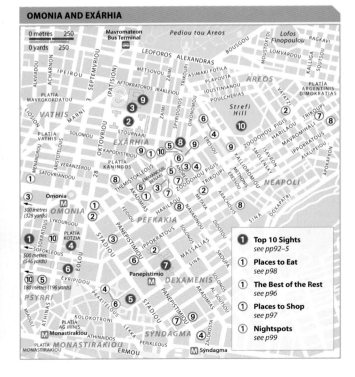

OMONIA AND EXÁRHIA

❶	**Top 10 Sights** see pp92–5
①	**Places to Eat** see p98
①	**The Best of the Rest** see p96
①	**Places to Shop** see p97
①	**Nightspots** see p99

Marble statue at the Polytechnic

headquarters of the National Bank of Greece. Next door to the bank is the more contemporary National Bank of Greece Cultural Centre, which was cleverly built to show off the remains of the ancient Acharnian Gate. Look out for the antiquities that were uncovered in the square, including tombs and part of an ancient road that once led out of the city.

2 Polytechnic
MAP C/D1–2

This is where the student demonstrations against the junta in 1973 (see p94) began. In front of the Polytechnic there is a marble statue of a youth's head lying on the ground – a monument to the fallen heroes of the uprising. Every year on 17 November, all of Greece's politicians turn out to put flowers at the memorial.

3 Epigraphical Museum
MAP D1 ▪ Tositsa 1
▪ 210 821 7637 ▪ Open 8am–3pm Tue–Sun

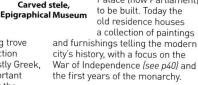

Carved stele, Epigraphical Museum

Housed here is a fascinating trove of Athenean lore. The collection comprises over 14,000, mostly Greek, inscriptions. The most important exhibits include a decree by the assembly of Athens ordering the evacuation of the city before the Persian invasion in 480 BC; a sacred law concerning temple-worship on the Acropolis; and a stele carved with accounts of the construction of the Erechtheion at the Acropolis in 421 BC.

4 Platía Kotzia
MAP C3

Lined with beautiful Neo-Classical buildings, this square is home to the Athens City Hall and the

5 Museum of the City of Athens Vouros-Eutaxias Foundation
MAP L2 ▪ Paparrigopoulou 7
▪ 210 323 1397 ▪ Open 9am–4pm Mon & Wed–Fri, 10am–3pm Sat & Sun ▪ Adm

This was the first house built in Athens after it was declared capital of the new kingdom of Greece in 1834. Otto, the country's first king, had it joined with next door, and lived here while he waited for the first Royal Palace (now Parliament) to be built. Today the old residence houses a collection of paintings and furnishings telling the modern city's history, with a focus on the War of Independence (see p40) and the first years of the monarchy.

Nikolaos Gyzis's *Carnival in Athens* **(1892), Museum of the City of Athens**

Nut stall, Central Market

6 Central Market (Varvakios Agora)

MAP K1/2 ■ Open 7am–3pm Mon–Sat

The enormous meat, fish and spice markets are a sensory overload that shouldn't be missed by any but the most squeamish. Several restaurants dot the meat market, serving until dawn. Outside, the air around the spice stores, centred on Athinas, is redolent with vanilla, saffron and dried mountain sage tea.

7 Athens University and Academy of Arts

MAP L/M1–2 ■ Panepistimiou

The city's university, the Academy of Arts and the National Library (see p96) make up a trio of the most important Neo-Classical buildings in Athens. The column bases and capitals of the university entrance are replicas of those in the Acropolis Propylaia, and the Academy entrance draws from the eastern side of the Erechtheion. The university's frescoes depict King Otto surrounded by personifications of the arts.

8 Platía Exárhia

MAP D2

While it may seem a bit threatening around the edges, but Platía Exárhia is a lively spot surrounded by many cafés favoured by an alternative crowd. The roads leading up to it are covered with politically charged graffiti and blanketed with posters advertising the latest demonstration. At the same time, the roads are fun to explore, lined with little independent shops selling all manner of records, vintage clothing and books. De rigueur

Athens University and Academy of Arts

frappé-sipping attire in the bars and cafés around here is unruly hair, piercings, ripped clothing, and messenger bags. At night it's an atmospheric place to be as the nightlife starts up.

9 National Archaeological Museum

This superb museum, often known simply as the National Museum (see pp20–21), opened in 1891, bringing together a collection that had previously been scattered across the city. With its unique exhibits, including an unrivalled amount of sculpture, pottery and jewellery, this is without doubt one of the world's finest museums.

National Archaeological Museum

10 Strefi Hill (Lofos Strefis)
MAP E1 ■ Anexartisias & Emmanouil Benaki

Strefi Hill is often overlooked by visitors due to its reputation as a druggie hangout by night. However, the hill is perfectly safe to visit during the day, where a short hike, popular with dog walkers, takes you up to a vantage point with spectacular views of the gritty neighbourhood of Omonia, Exárhia, the Lykavittos Hill, the Acropolis and beyond. Just be sure to leave before dark.

A DAY AROUND OMONIA

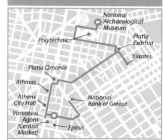

▶ MORNING

Start at Greece's greatest treasure storehouse: the **National Archaeological Museum**. Don't miss the Mycenean Treasure, Thera Frescoes and Classical statuary.

When leaving the museum, turn left on Patission, noting the nearby **Polytechnic** (see p93), scene of 1973's historic protests. Outside the building, a giant marble head lies on the ground, a memorial to the fallen students.

Turn left on Stournari, and make your way to **Platía Exárhia** for a frappé and to watch the university students go by. In summer, head to **Yiantes** (see p98) for an alfresco lunch.

AFTERNOON

Travel downhill on Themistokleous. Walk quickly past the historic but chaotic and seedy **Platía Omonia** on **Athinas**. Once beyond here you'll pass the stately **Athens City Hall** (see p96) on your right before turning left onto Sofokleous. Go down this street to see the **National Bank of Greece**, built on stilts over part of the Themistoklean Wall. Across Eolou, the archaeological digs lie exposed.

Double back to get to the city's real heart – the **Varvakios Agora (Central Market)**. Lose yourself in the sights, sounds and smells of the stalls. Just one market taverna has survived the economic crisis: **Epirus**, famous for its *patsas* (tripe soup), the classic Greek hangover cure.

See map on p92

The Best of the Rest

1 National Theatre
**MAP B2 ▪ Agiou Konstantinou
22–4 ▪ 210 528 8170 ▪ www.n-t.gr/en**
The majestic outlines of Hadrian's
Library served as the model for this
fine Neo-Classical building's façade.
Performances by the National
Theatre troupe are Greece's best.

National Library

2 National Library
**MAP L1 ▪ Panepistimiou 32
▪ Open 9am–8pm Mon–Thu,
9am–2pm Fri & Sat ▪ www.nlg.gr**
One of the important Neo-Classical
trio of downtown buildings (see p94).
The reading room is exceptional. The
library is slowly relocating to the Stavros
Niarchos Foundation Cultural Centre.

3 Rebecca Camhi Gallery
**MAP B2 ▪ Leonidou 9 ▪ Open
noon–6pm Tue (until 8pm Wed–Fri),
visits by appointment at other
times ▪ www.rebeccacamhi.com**
This gallery presents both Greek
and foreign contemporary artists.

4 Agii Theodoroi
**MAP K2 ▪ Plateia Agion
Theodoron**
A tiny, peaceful 11th-century church
in the bustle of the marketplace.
The wall paintings are 19th century.

5 CHEAPART Athens
**MAP D2 ▪ Andrea Metaxa 25
▪ www.cheapart.gr**
A not-for-profit art space that hosts
exhibitions by contemporary Greek
and international artists. It promotes
the work of emerging artists as well.

6 Ianos
MAP L2 ▪ Stadiou 24
This notable bookstore mainly
stocks books in Greek language.
Its main attraction is the excellent
café and the event venue on the
top floor that hosts book launches
as well as concerts.

7 Grigoropoulos Shrine
MAP D2 ▪ Tzavella
Teenager Alexandros Grigoropoulos
was shot by the police in December
2008. Three days of riots ensued.
A plaque, flowers and candles
are dedicated to him.

8 Athens City Hall
MAP J1 ▪ Athinas 63
The headquarters for managing
Greater Athens' 40 separate
municipalities. The archaeological
dig in front reveals an area just
outside Athens' old city walls.

9 Odos Kallidromiou
MAP D2
Come to the colourful Saturday
street market here for a real feel
of the vibrant Exárhia community.

10 Agios Nikolaos Pefkakia
MAP E2 ▪ Asklipeiou
Built in 1895, the church of Agios
Nikolaos Pefkakia (St Nicholas
of the Pines) crowns the top of
steep Dervenion Street.

Church of Agios Nikolaos Pefkakia

Places to Shop

Loumidis Coffee Shop

1 Loumidis Coffee Shop
MAP M2 ▪ Panepistimiou 69

This vast corner coffee shop (*see p68*) specializes in traditional Greek coffee, selling a selection of *brikia* (coffee pots) in which to boil it, cups and saucers, and sweet treats.

2 Miran
MAP K2 ▪ Evripidou 45

Set up by Armenian refugees in 1922, this shop offers fantastic *pastourma* (cured veal or camel) and *soutzouki* (spicy veal salami).

3 Stoa tou Vivliou
MAP C3 ▪ Pesmazoglou 5 & Stadiou

In the commercial heart of Athens, this tranquil arcade with old-world charm houses bookshops, binders and antiquarian outlets.

4 Zoumboulakis Gallery
MAP M3 ▪ Kriezotou 6 ▪ www.zoumboulakis.gr

This celebrated art gallery and shop has a spectacular selection of original paintings and signed, numbered prints by many of Greece's finest artists.

5 Politeia
MAP D2 ▪ Asklipiou 1–3

Bookshops have become rare in Greece, but Politeia is a thriving store with three separate entrances. Come here to check out their foreign language books and CDs.

6 Xylouris
MAP L1
▪ Stoa Pesmazoglou, Panepistimiou 39

Named after the late singer Nikos Xylouris, this store is a treasure house of traditional Greek music and rare CDs.

7 Zolotas
MAP M2
▪ Panepistimiou 10 ▪ www.zolotqasjewelery.com

Known for its intricate creations in hammered gold, Zolotas is one of Athens' most treasured brands.

8 Nakas Musical Instruments
MAP D2/3 ▪ Navarinou 13 & Mavromihali

Five floors of musical items, from inlaid *bouzoukia* to violins, sheet music, DJ decks and loudspeakers.

Bouzoukia on sale in a store

9 Karavan
MAP M2 ▪ Voukourestiou 11

Choose from the scrumptious *baklavas* and *kataifi* at this tiny but deservedly popular alcove of a shop.

10 Music Corner
MAP C3 ▪ Panepistimiou 56

A vast selection of Greek and East Mediterranean sounds, as well as classical music and jazz, blues and rock CDs.

See map on p92 ←

Places to Eat

1 Tivoli
MAP D2 ▪ Emmanouil Benaki 34 ▪ 210 383 0919 ▪ €

This *mezedopolio* is also a live music venue. It offers regional dishes from Skopelos and affordable drinks.

2 Warehouse
MAP D2 ▪ Valtetsiou 21 & Mavromihali ▪ €

Choose from 30 wines by the glass, or 50 by the bottle, at this industrial-style bar. It is known for its coffee and light midday snacks.

The well-stocked bar at Warehouse

3 Salero
MAP D2 ▪ Valtetsiou 51 ▪ 210 381 3358 ▪ €

Open until 2am, this place serves Mediterranean tapas, cheese platters and desserts.

4 Yiantes
MAP D2 ▪ Valtetsiou 44 ▪ 210 330 1369 ▪ €

Exárhia's poshest taverna offers creative versions of Greek and Mediterranean dishes. Ingredients are produced organically.

5 Rozalia
MAP D2 ▪ Valtetsiou 58 ▪ 210 330 216 ▪ €

Waiters present a giant tray of *mezedes* (small plates) to choose from. They also offer outdoor seating in the courtyard during summers.

> **PRICE CATEGORIES**
> For a three-course meal for one with half a bottle of wine (or equivalent meal), taxes and extra charges.
>
> € under €40 €€ €40–€60 €€€ over €60

6 Ama Lahei
MAP D1 ▪ Kallidromiou 69 ▪ 210 384 5978 ▪ €

Set in an old house, this place has a large tiered garden. Wash down the food with *raki* served by the carafe.

7 Peinaleon
MAP E1 ▪ Mavromihali 152 ▪ 210 644 0945 ▪ Open Oct–May ▪ €

Founded 1975, this taverna has an antique-crammed interior. Enjoy the hearty food in an atmospheric setting.

8 I Kriti
MAP C2 ▪ Veranzerou 5 ▪ €

Set in an arcade this place serves up Cretan platters and sausages, along with Sitian wine.

9 Klimataria
MAP J1 ▪ Platía Theatrou 2 ▪ 210 321 6629 ▪ €

In a seedy part of Omonia stands this warm, old-world taverna, known for its acoustic rembetika music.

10 Rififi
MAP D2 ▪ Emmanouil Benaki 69A & Valtetsiou ▪ 210 330 0237 ▪ €

This contemporary taverna offers creative dishes such as paparadelle with mushrooms and truffle oil, or pork neck in balsamic ginger sauce.

Pastel-coloured interior of Rififi

Nightspots

The rock band Biohazard performing at An Club

① An Club
MAP C2 ■ Solomou 13–15
■ www.anclub.gr

One of Athens' oldest and best-loved live music clubs, showcasing rock and alternative bands. Rave parties continue well after 1am. Check their website to see who is performing.

② Makari
MAP E1 ■ Pigis 125 & Komninon ■ 210 645 8958

This bar arranges performances by rembetika bands twice a month, which are often led by Yiorgos Makris. Book in advance.

③ Beatniks Road Bar
MAP D2 ■ Koletti 14

Enjoy DJd, live blues and rock music at this bar. The walls are decorated with various homages to beatnik, early rock and jazz culture.

④ Efimeron
MAP D2 ■ Methonis 58
■ 210 384 1848

Located on a quiet back street, this excellent taverna offers a varied menu. From 10pm onwards it plays host to acoustic rembetika musicians.

⑤ Tivoli Live
MAP D2 ■ Emmanouil Benaki 34 ■ 210 383 0919

Established rembetika stars perform here. Book in advance as there are limited seats.

⑥ Alexandrino
MAP D2 ■ Emmanouil Benaki 69 A

A local favourite, this small café-bistro is famous for its excellent wines and cocktails as well as teas.

⑦ Off The Chain
MAP D2 ■ Zoödohou Pigis 25

This bar plays alternative rock, indie and industrial music. It fills up late (after 3am) and parties till sunrise at weekends.

⑧ Rembetiki Istoria
MAP E2 ■ Ippokratous 181
■ 210 642 4937 ■ Open Oct–May

This bar, tucked into an early 20th-century building, has original moulded walls and ceilings.

⑨ Boemissa
MAP C2 ■ Solomou 13–15
■ 210 383 8803

This is a great place to enjoy authentic live rembetika music while dining on traditional Greek dishes. You can also just have drinks.

⑩ Ginger Ale
MAP D2 ■ Themistokleous 74

Decorated with flowered wallpaper and vintage posters, this café and cocktail-bar overlooks Exárhia Square. It's a popular after-theatre haunt for actors who come to enjoy the sounds of soul and jazz over drinks.

See map on p92

TOP 10 Syndagma and Kolonaki

Plateia Syndagma, the centre of modern Athens, is crowned by the large, Neo-Classical Parliament building. Standing sentry outside are the *evzones* (soldiers) marching solemnly back and forth in traditional kilts and *tsarouhia* (pompommed shoes). Along the Vouli's north flank begins the avenue Vasilissis Sofias is Museum Row, where many of Athens' finest museums are concentrated. Beyond Vasilissis Sofias lies posh Kolonaki, home to ambassadors, models, movie stars and the fabulous designer boutiques that cater to them. This is the prime spot for shopping, people-watching and pricey café-sitting. Rising above it all is Lykavittos Hill, topped by a famous outdoor theatre, cafés and a restaurant with a view to die for.

Evzone guard in traditional attire

SYNDAGMA AND KOLONAKI

1 Kallimarmaro Stadium

MAP N6 ■ Vas Konstantinou
■ **Open Mar–Oct: 8am–7pm; Nov–Feb: 8am–5pm daily**

Also known as the Panathenaic, the Kallimarmaro (meaning "beautiful marble") (see p61) was first built in 330 BC for the Panathenaic games, and later fell into disuse. In 1895, George Averoff had it restored with fine Pentelic marble, and it hosted the first modern Olympics in 1896. In 2004, it provided the final circuit for the Olympic Marathon and also hosted the archery competition. It is still used for concerts and other events.

2 National Gardens

MAP M4 ■ Amalias

The huge, shady National Gardens are an unexpected green refuge in parched central Athens. They were originally planted in 1839 as the Royal Garden of Queen Amalia, who had her horticulturalists (and the Greek fleet) bring in 15,000 domestic and exotic plants, many of which are still alive. The garden was opened to the public in 1923. It has a small, run down zoo, two duck ponds, free-ranging tortoises and a playground.

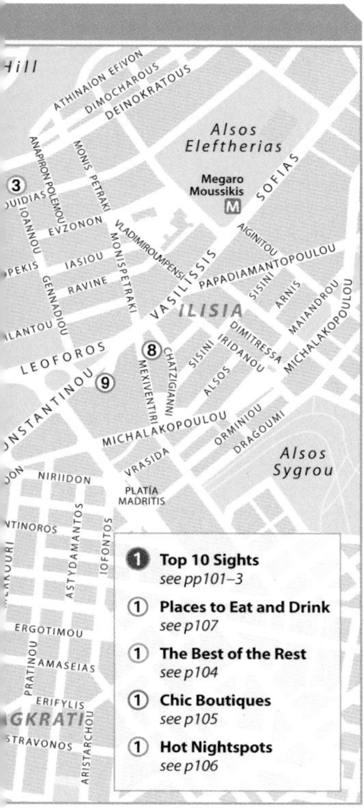

3 National Parliament Building

MAP M3 ■ Platía Syndagmatos
■ **Library: Open 9am–2pm, 5:30–8:30pm Mon–Fri, 9am–2pm Sat**

The imposing building was erected in 1842 as a palace for King Otto. Over the next 70 years, it suffered neglect, and in 1923, it served as a shelter for refugees from Asia Minor. In 1926, after the return of parliamentary government, the building was gutted, renovated and re-opened as a single-chamber council for parliament. Today it is the scene of debates that range from the surreal to the more mundane. Its library can be visited.

National Parliament Building

4 Syndagma Metro Station

MAP M3

Syndagma station (see p44) is as much museum as transport hub. When the city was busy excavating to extend the metro, archaeologists found thousands of priceless items on this site, which has been continuously occupied since Classical times. Many are displayed in the station, but the highlight is a glass wall overlooking the site, which includes at least two cemeteries.

Lykavittos Hill and the neighbourhood of Kolonaki

5 Lykavittos Hill
MAP F2

Steep Lykavittos Hill juts high out of Kolonaki, and the church at its peak is visible for miles around. Every summer, the Lykavittos Festival hosts a variety of top musicians from around the world in the theatre beyond the church; there's nothing like watching Bob Dylan with the sun going down over Athens behind them. A smart café-restaurant nestles below the church. If you are very, very ambitious, walk up – otherwise, take the funicular from Aristippou.

6 Benaki Museum

The Benaki (see pp26–7) is one of Greece's pre-eminent museums, not only for its extensive and impressive collection of

Icon of The Raising of Lazaros, Benaki Museum

ZILLER THE THRILLER

Shortly after the Kingdom of Greece was established in 1832, Neo-Classicism became the dominant architectural style in Athens. Ernst Ziller was its foremost practitioner, who designed more than 500 buildings across Greece. Ziller's Neo-Classicism can be seen in the Cycladic Museum, the Numismatic Museum (see p104) and the National Theatre.

prehistoric to 20th-century Greek art, but also because it's a lovely place to be. Among its highlights are the re-creations of Ottoman-style sitting rooms in 18th-century northern Greek mansions, and Byzantine shrines. The superb books and jewellery in the gift shop and the rooftop garden restaurant are destinations in themselves.

7 Museum of Cycladic Art

Some 2,000 years before the Parthenon, a mysterious civilization on the Cycladic islands created the prototypical Mediterranean marble sculptures: simple, and mostly elemental female forms. The figures still resonate today, famously influencing artists such as Modigliani, Moore and Picasso (see pp22–3). The Goulandris family, one of Greece's oldest shipping and philanthropic dynasties, displays the world's largest collection of Cycladic art in a building erected in 1985 by the architect Ioannis Vikelas. There are often exhibits by top contemporary Greek and international artists in the extra-swanky exhibition wing.

War Museum
MAP E/F4 ■ Vas Sofias & Rizari
2 ■ 210 725 2974 ■ Open Nov–Mar:
9am–5pm daily (Apr–Oct: until 7pm)

The two huge floors telling the
history of warfare in Greece (see
p49) from prehistoric to modern
times are compelling. The museum
comprises uniforms, weaponry of all
eras and diplomatic documents on
Greece's trials during World War II.
Outside stand two fighter planes and
a few 20th-century artillery pieces.

**9 Byzantine and
Christian Museum**

The museum's (see pp32–3) collection
dates from the 3rd to the 19th centuries, chronicling the rise and fall of
the Byzantine Empire and its influence
on the areas which would become
Greece. There are sculptures, icons
and religious trappings in gold and
silver. It is housed in a two-level
space built partially under ground.

Byzantine and Christian Museum

10 Evzones
MAP M3 ■ Changing of the
Guard every hour

On guard in front of Parliament are
the famous *evzones*, soldiers in the
traditional attire of the rebels who won
the War of Independence. It's hard to
imagine fighting efficiently in this uni-
form: a short white skirt (with 400
pleats, symbolizing the years under
Ottoman rule), red cap and *tsarouhia*
(pompommed shoes). The Changing
of the Guard is like a slow high-kick
dance. *Evzones* are selected from the
tallest and most handsome men in
the mandatory Greek military service.
The best time to watch is on Sunday,
at 11 am in the morning.

AN AFTERNOON IN CHIC KOLONAKI

MID-AFTERNOON

Start at **Platía Syndagmatos**
a few minutes before the hour
to see the Changing of the
Guard in front of the **Tomb of
the Unknown Soldier**. Then
head up **Vasilissis Sofias** to
the **Museum of Cycladic Art**
to ponder the mysterious prehistoric marble sculptures.
Check out whatever temporary
exhibition is on at the adjoining
Stathatos Mansion – they are
usually world-class shows.

Then it's on to **Platía Kolonakiou**
for a frappé and a pastry at
one of the cafés along the
Tsakalof pedestrian way and
some people-watching. The
parade of wealthy wives, pretty
playboys and Greek starlets
provides recompense for the
overpriced drinks – sip slowly!

LATE AFTERNOON

For lunch, head to **Taverna
Filippou** at Xenokratous 19.
Afterwards, fan out from
the square for some serious
shopping or browsing of the
shop windows and eyeing
patrons at Kalogirou – **Boho**
and **Twisted Classics** (see
p105), as well as familiar international staples such as Gucci,
Armani and Balenciaga.

Towards the end of the day, go
to the **Funicular Station** at the
foot of **Lykavittos Hill**. From
the hilltop at dusk, watch the
sky turn violet over Athens, while
enjoying a drink at the café, or
a truly special meal at **Orizontes**
restaurant (see p107).

The Best of the Rest

① Zappeion
MAP M5

The Zappeion designed by Theophil Hansen in 1874, stands in pleasant grounds at the southern end of the National Gardens. Its tree-lined paths are open to the public, while the Zappeion itself hosts various events.

National Historical Museum

② National Historical Museum
MAP L2 ■ Stadiou 13, Platía Kolokotroni ■ Open 8:30am–2:30pm Tue–Sun ■ Adm ■ www.nhmuseum.gr

Greece's first parliament building is now a museum specializing in the Independence war. It features displays on the fall of Byzantium, the Latin and Ottoman rule, and holds excellent temporary exhibitions.

③ Gennadeion Library
MAP F3 ■ Souidias 61 ■ Open 9am–5pm Mon, Tue, Wed & Fri, 9am–8pm Thu, 9am–2pm Sat ■ www.ascsa.edu.gr

Now part of the American School of Classical Studies, this library of multilingual volumes is one of the world's best resources for all things Hellenic.

④ Presidential Palace
MAP N4 ■ Between Irodou Attikou & Meleagrou

The former palace of King Constantine I was designed by Ernst Ziller (see p102) from 1891–97.

⑤ Numismatic Museum/ Schliemann's House
MAP M2 ■ Panepistimiou 12 ■ Open 8:30am–3:30pm Tue–Sun ■ Adm

This coin collection is housed in the mansion of Heinrich Schliemann, discoverer of the Mycenae treasure.

⑥ Museum of the History of Greek Costume
MAP M2 ■ Dimokritou 7 ■ Open 10am–2pm Mon–Fri ■ Closed Aug

Over 6,000 items of clothing, jewellery and adornments showing the variety of Greek dress through the ages.

⑦ Platía Kolonakiou
MAP N3

A pleasant square with plenty of cafés nearby where you can grab a drink.

⑧ Platía Dexameni
MAP N/P2

Greener and lower-key than Platía Kolonakiou, and home to one of Athens' nicest outdoor cinemas.

⑨ Friday Morning Street Market
MAP P2 ■ Xenokratous

This is one of Athens' most lively outdoor fruit and vegetable markets.

⑩ Tomb of the Unknown Soldier
MAP M3 ■ Platía Syndagmatos

A relief carving of a dying gunner, (see p40) carved by sculptor Fokion Rok in 1930–32, adorns this cenotaph commemorating Greece's war dead since the Independence war.

Tomb of the Unknown Soldier

Chic Boutiques

The minimalist interior of Folli Follie

1 Folli Follie
MAP L3 ■ Ermou 19

Attractive, high-quality and affordably priced watches, necklaces, bracelets, bags and other accessories.

2 Dassios
MAP P3 ■ Vasilissis Sofias 35

Dimitris Dassios creates extravagant but tasteful denim-wear, jackets, bags and jewellery from silk and leather, with ornamental details.

3 Oikos
MAP E4 ■ Irodotou 26

The most contemporary designs in Greece are showcased at this expensive store selling furniture, lighting and accessories.

4 Twisted Classics
MAP E4 ■ Irodotou 29

New collections of made-to-measure and ready-to-wear garments are created every month by owner/designer Katia Delatola using beautiful hand-drawn prints.

5 Lena Katsanidou Clothing
MAP P2/3 ■ Loukianou 21

Lena Katsanidou's Kolonaki boutique and upstairs atelier sells highly desirable items, including her signature line of patterned and hued summer outfits.

6 Graffito
MAP M2 ■ Solonos 34

This is a first concept emporium that has a diverse collection of clothing, accessories and furnishings from Greece and around the world.

7 Boho
MAP P3 ■ Karneadou 15 & Loukianou

Christianna Verouka is known for her upmarket 70s-inspired clothing – floaty scarves, chunky jewellery and leather shoulder bags – perfect for Greek island summer nightlife.

8 Elena Votsi
MAP N/P2 ■ Xanthou 7

A popular name on the international jewellery circuit, Votsi does chunky, rough-edged investment pieces that are worth every penny.

9 Kalogirou
MAP P2 ■ Patriarhou Ioakeim 4

Stocks an overwhelming array of designer shoes and a wide selection of Kalogirou's own stylish creations.

10 Bettina
MAP N2 ■ Panagiotou Anagnostopoulou 29

Bettina's impressive stock includes international labels alongside Greece's own Angelos Frentzos and Sophia Kokosalaki.

See map on pp100–101

Hot Nightspots

Galaxy Bar, offering fine views and upmarket surroundings

1 Black Duck Multiplarte
MAP D4 ■ Christou Lada 9a, Syndagma

With duck-themed wall art, DJ evenings and 1960s–70s rock music on the soundtrack, it's the after-dark iteration of a daytime garden bistro.

2 Skoufaki
MAP M1 ■ Skoufa 47–9

Small, dimly lit, smoky and full of artists and actor types, Skoufaki is Kolonaki's most famous, longest-established alternative café and bar.

3 Milioni Street
MAP N3

This street's fairy lights attract the youth of Kolonaki until the early hours, as do the many bars and cafés, such as Jackson Hall, a combo bar and American-themed diner at No. 4.

4 Minnie the Moocher
MAP N2 ■ Tsakalof 6

Set on Kolonaki's posh pedestrian strip, this 1930s-style hotspot serves a range of great cocktails, with jazz and swing music often playing.

5 Seven Jokers
MAP L4 ■ Voulis 7

This café-bar aims to re-create the atmosphere of 1920s Paris. Huge sandwiches help to absorb the vast amounts of alcohol served.

6 Galaxy Bar
MAP F4 ■ Vasilissis Sofias 46
■ 210 728 1402

On the top floor of the Hilton, this slick, partly open-air bar serves signature cocktails, sushi and finger food. At night, it offers stunning views over the city.

7 Rock 'n' Roll
MAP E4 ■ Loukianou 6

An old Kolonaki favourite, this operates out of its original 1987 location. Enjoy the atmosphere of a slightly older crowd and the booze.

8 Drunk Sinatra
MAP L3 ■ Thiseos 16

This colourful and trendy vintage bar hosts a lively crowd that often spills out onto the pedestrian street.

9 The Clumsies
MAP K2 ■ Praxitelous 30

Set in a Neo-Classical mansion from 1919, this popular bar with a wooden beamed ceiling and striking decor serves great cocktails, light snacks and Sunday brunch.

10 Jazz in Jazz
MAP P2 ■ Dinokratous 4

Somewhat hard to find (it's off Platia Dexamenis), this tiny bar has a jazz soundtrack, low lighting and a fine range of whiskies, rums and beers.

Places to Eat and Drink

PRICE CATEGORIES
For a three-course meal for one with half a bottle of wine (or equivalent meal), taxes and extra charges.
....
€ under €40 €€ €40–€60 €€€ over €60

1  **Orizontes**
MAP P1 ■ Aristippou 1
■ 210 721 0701 ■ €€€
Enjoy a view of the capital while dining on creative Greek cuisine and risotto/pasta dishes atop Lykavittos Hill.

2 Kiku
MAP N2 ■ Dimokritou 12
■ 210 364 7033 ■ €€€
This Japanese restaurant (dinner only) has an impeccable selection of mostly seafood and desserts.

3 Spondi
MAP E6 ■ Pyrronos 5
■ 210 756 4021 ■ €€€
Upmarket French cuisine with Greek references – think crab, langoustine and milk-fed lamb. Only dinner is served.

4 Mouries
MAP E6 ■ Platia Varnava and Krisila, Pangrati ■ 210 701 6100 ■ €
For a specialist in *magirefta* (casserole dishes), head to Mouries, especially for lunch. Tables are set inside and out, under namesake mulberries.

5 Winter Garden
MAP M3 ■ Vasileos Georgiou 1, Platia Syndagmatos ■ 210 333 0000 ■ €€€
Enjoy a European breakfast, light lunch, high tea or dinner at this restaurant in the luxurious Hotel Grande Bretagne.

6 Il Postino
MAP D3 ■ Griveon 3, off Skoufa
■ 210 364 1414 ■ €
This genuine, Italian-run *osteria* serves pasta dishes (20 choices daily), salads and a few heartier mains, plus of course tiramisu, in a very quiet setting.

7  **Oikeio**
MAP E4 ■ Plutarhou 15
■ 210 725 9216 ■ €€
This bistro with objet-trouve decor has all the Greek staples including less common ones such as sauteed rabbit. Reservations are suggested; service is friendly.

8 Cookoovaya
MAP F4 ■ Hatzigianni Mexi 2a
■ 210 723 5005 ■ €€€
The daily changing menu here offers salads, grilled grouper with orzo, fennel and botarga, or fresh hake with artichokes, beans, peas and fennel.

Well-lit dining room at Milos

9 Milos
MAP F4 ■ Vasilissis Sofias 46
■ 210 724 4400 ■ €€€
At the Hilton, Milos has Mediterranean cuisine emphasising on seafood and raw fish, with Black Angus fillet on offer for those who prefer meat.

10 Mikri Vouli
MAP E6 ■ Platia Varnava 8, Pangrati ■ 210 756 5523 ■ €€
The only *mezedopolio* around this square, this has excellent affordable *tsipouro* (distilled grape pomace spirit) by the *karafaki* (glass flagon) and meat, fish or vegetable platters.

See map on pp100–101

🔟 Piraeus

Renowned for seedy cafés, the city's port, Piraeus, is the main gateway from Athens to the islands. The port of Athens since ancient times, it was redeveloped after independence. Islanders from Hios, Ydra and Syros set up the first factories, joined by an influx of refugees from Asia Minor in 1923. It soon became Greece's main industrial centre, and is now the third-largest Mediterranean port. COSCO Shipping from China, has been the majority shareholder of Piraeus port since 2016.

Hellenic Maritime Museum

① Hellenic Maritime Museum

Akti Themistokleous, Freattyda ■ **210 428 6959** ■ **Open 9am–2pm Tue–Sat (until 1:30pm Sun & Mon)** ■ **Adm**

Housed in a 1960s building at the mouth of Zea Marina, this exhibition opens with a map of Odysseus's voyage across the Mediterranean. It then traces the history of Greek naval trading, with models of ships ranging

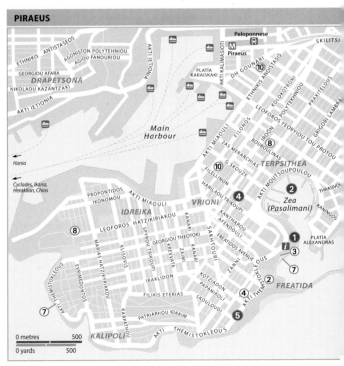

PIRAEUS

from the 5th-century BC trireme (see p54) to modern tankers (Greece has the largest merchant fleet in the world). Naval warfare is covered by massive oil paintings of historic sea battles against the Ottomans.

Peace and Friendship Stadium

2 Zea (Pasalimani)
This large bay, with a bottleneck channel opening out to the sea, is surrounded by tall apartment blocks. Inaugurated as Athens' main naval base in the 5th century BC, the ancient harbour of Marina Zea could accommodate 196 triremes. Today, up to 400 of the most impressive motor yachts in Greece moor here. It takes about 20 minutes to walk the perimeter of the bay, along a tree-lined promenade overlooked by tavernas and cafés.

3 Peace and Friendship Stadium
Tram Terminus Stadio Irinis ke Filias
Close to Faliro metro station, this bowl-shaped enclosed arena hosts international competitions in basketball, volleyball and wrestling, and was a venue during the 2004 Olympics. It is also used for rock concerts.

4 Archaeological Museum of Piraeus
Harilaou Trikoupi 32 ■ 210 452 1598 ■ 8am–3pm Tue–Sun ■ Closed Aug and public hols ■ Adm
Built by the remains of the 2nd-century BC Theatre of Zea, the showpieces here are two classical bronze statues: the perfectly proportioned 5th-century BC Piraeus Apollo and the 4th-century BC Piraeus Athena. Also on display is a collection of 5th- and 4th-century BC marble *stelai* (Classical gravestones) with touching reliefs of the deceased.

Saronic Gulf

1 **Top 10 Sights**
see pp108–11

1 **Places to Eat**
see p112

1 **Bars and Cafés**
see p113

Archaeological Museum of Piraeus

(5) Akti Themistokleous

From Freattyda, a 3-km- (2-mile-) long coastal promenade, overlooked by apartment blocks and a string of informal fish restaurants, offers wonderful views across the open sea to the islands of Egina and Salamina. The route, named after the 5th-century BC general and statesman Themistokles, who founded Piraeus, follows the course of the ancient sea-ward walls. Down below, a series of rocky bays offers sunbathing. The prettiest spot of all is Aphrodite's Bay.

(6) Kastella

Built into the northern and eastern sides of the Profitis Ilias hill, which overlooks Mikrolimano, this picturesque residential quarter is filled with pastel-coloured Neo-Classical houses, built between 1834 and 1900, and a labyrinth of steep streets and stairways. There's a village atmosphere here, making it a great area to explore on foot. The highest point is crowned with the church of Profitis Ilias, which offers spectacular views of Athens, while on the southern slope the small open-air Veakeio Theatre is used for staging delightful summer performances.

(7) Yacht Club of Greece
Mikrolimano

Europe's top destination for yachters, thanks to its myriad islands, Greece has a 3,500-year tradition of sailing.

Yacht Club of Greece

Mikrolimano's bay

Set in landscaped gardens on a peninsula on the south side of Mikrolimano, the yacht club was founded in 1934. The main clubhouse is the province of members only, but you can stroll around the marina, then stop for a drink at the chic rooftop bar, Istioploïkos (see p113).

Battleship Averof

(8) Battleship Averof
Trokadero Marina, Paleo Faliro
■ **210 988 8211** ■ **Open 9am–2pm Tue–Fri, 10am–5pm Sat & Sun** ■ **Adm**

Built in Livorno (Italy) in 1910, this 140-m- (460-ft-) long battleship was designed to carry 670 men in peacetime and 1,200 during war, and led the Greek fleet through the Balkan Wars and World Wars I and II. Negotiating a series of narrow ladders, you can explore the entire ship, from the kitchen and engine rooms to the main bridge, from the cramped dark space where the crew slept in hammocks, to the contrasting luxury of the officers' mess and the Admiral's sumptuous wood-panelled suite.

A DAY IN PIRAEUS

9 Mikrolimano

Best known for its fish restaurants with open-air waterside terraces, this delightful circular bay is built on a human scale. The ancients believed it was protected by the goddess Artemis, and initially named it after the Mounihia festival. The Ottoman navy used it too, which is why it is still sometimes known as Tourkolimano (Turkish harbour). Today it is filled with the small wooden boats of local fishermen, who supply the surrounding restaurants from their daily catch.

10 Karaïskakis Stadium

MAP T2 ∎ Karaoli Dimitriou & Sofianopoulou

Home ground to Olympiakos Football Club, this stadium was reconstructed for the 2004 Olympics and painted red after the club's strip. With a capacity of 33,000 spectators, besides staging Superleague Greece and big international matches, it occasionally hosts rock concerts. You'll find it next to Faliro metro station.

LION OF PIRAEUS

In medieval times the main port of Piraeus was known as Porto Leone in tribute to a 3-m- (10-ft-) tall marble lion that stood on the site of the present Town Hall. In 1687, the Venetians carried it off and placed it in the Arsenale in Venice. A copy of the original stands on Akti Favierou, visible from approaching ferries.

MORNING/AFTERNOON

From Athens, take the metro to Piraeus, then walk to the **Archaeological Museum** (see p109) and check out some of the ancient local finds.

Continue to **Zea (Pasalimani)** and stop for a coffee at **Moby** (see p113), overlooking the water. Take the time for a stroll around the harbour to admire the top-notch boats.

For a relaxed lunch, call at **Imerovigli** (see p112), which offers fantastic sea views; otherwise, walk the seafront promenade of **Akti Themistokleous** for a reasonably priced informal feast of fresh fish at **Margaro** (see p112).

EVENING

Take the metro to Faliro, then negotiate a busy main road past the **Peace and Friendship Stadium** (see p109), one of Piraeus's venues that was used during the 2004 Olympic Games.

Continue southwest from the stadium to arrive at the pretty fishing harbour of **Mikrolimano** – more picturesque than the more central bays.

Here you'll find a string of waterside seafood restaurants, among which **Dourabeis** is a reliable choice (see p112).

After dinner, either escape for a romantic nightcap at hillside **Don Quixote** in Kastella (see p113) or join the crowds at **Istioploïkos** (see p113), one of the café-bars with brash music and open-air seating on Akti Koumoundourou.

See map on pp108–9 ←

Places to Eat

PRICE CATEGORIES
For a three-course meal for one with half a bottle of wine (or equivalent meal), taxes and extra charges.

€ under €40   €€ €40–€60   €€€ over €60

1 Varoulko Seaside
Akti Koumoundourou 52, Mikrolimano ▪ 210 522 8400 ▪ €€€
Michelin-starred chef Lefteris Lazarou serves seafood delights such as squid with pesto, and red mullet in lemon sauce. They offer a tasting menu as well as à la carte.

2 Dourabeis
Akti Dilaveri 29, Mikrolimano ▪ 210 412 2092 ▪ €€€
Since 1933, Dourabeis has charmed diners with its sublime fresh fish and shellfish, simply grilled and dressed with lemon and olive oil.

3 Jimmy's Fish & the Sushi Tavern
Akti Koumoundourou 46, Mikrolimano ▪ 210 412 4417 ▪ €€€
Platters of smoked tuna and rocket, pans of lobster, and trays of sushi are served at the harbourside terrace.

4 Imerovigli
Akti Themistokleous 56, Freattyda ▪ 210 452 3382 ▪ €
Excellent seafood, with limited meat choices, accompanied by Greek wines, *ouzo*, *tsipouro* and beers. They host live performances.

5 Ammos
Akti Koumoundourou 44, Mikrolimano ▪ 210 433 4633 ▪ €
Located next to the sea, this casual *mezedopoleion* serves traditional meat and fish dishes.

6 Kapilio O Zahos
Komotinis 37, Piraeus ▪ 210 481 3325 ▪ €
This family-run taverna serves meat and seafood dishes. The interior befits a *kapilio* (wine tavern).

7 Diasimos
Akti Themistokleous 306–8, Piraïki ▪ 210 451 7471 ▪ €
Two blue-fronted buildings comprise this *psarotaverna* (fish eatery) founded in the 1960s. It has a selected wine and beer list and offers views of passing ferries from the seafront terrace.

8 Margaro
Hatzikyriakou 126 ▪ 210 451 4226 ▪ Closed Sun dinner and two weeks in Aug ▪ No credit cards ▪ €
Diners here enjoy a menu that includes salad, seafood as well as beer or wine. Dishes are prepared with the fresh catch of the day.

9 Papaïoannou
Akti Koumoundourou 42, Mikrolimano ▪ 210 422 5059 ▪ €€
Noted for its fresh seafood supplied directly from spear-fishers, chef Giorgos Papaïoannou presents creative dishes. The side platters include baby tomato salad, smoked eel as well as oysters.

10 Stoa Rakadiko
Karaoli Dimitriou 5, Stoa Kouvelou ▪ 210 417 8470 ▪ €
With a quirky decor, this place offers some unusual dishes made with buffalo meat. It is an excellent choice before or after a ferry ride.

Vibrant interiors of Stoa Rakadiko

Bars and Cafés

(1) Istioploïkos
Akti Mikrolimano
■ 210 413 4084 ■ Open mid-Mar–early Nov

One of the hip places to see and be seen, this vast rooftop bar commands a vantage point above the yachting marina.

Pizza platter at Moby

(2) Pisina
Akti Themistokleous 25, Freattyda ■ 210 451 1324

Centred around an open-air swimming pool, this modern bar-restaurant is stylish but relaxed.

(3) Rockfellas Excelsior
Marina Zeas ■ 210 418 4440

With walls covered by posters of well-known musicians, a bar lined with high stools, and leather sofas for lounging on, this place serves draught beer and cocktails. It hosts popular summer parties on Sundays.

(4) Don Quixote
Alexandrou Papanastasiou 68, Kastella

A hillside café-bar with a roof terrace offers great views of the open sea.

(5) Mecca
Akti Koumoundourou 62, Mikrolimano ■ 210 422 0138

Hot drinks, good food and cocktails can be had amid the modern architecture of this place with great views of the coast around Athens.

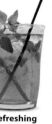

Refreshing Cocktail

(6) Bizz Café Lounge Bar
Akti Koumoundourou 8, Mikrolimano ■ 210 411 5344

With sofas, pouffes and coffee tables on a wooden deck that goes right up to the water's edge, this place is one of a string of lounge-cafés overlooking Mikrolimano.

(7) Moby
Marina Zeas ■ 211 012 3778

Locals come here for coffee and cocktails, as well as views of the sea. Moby runs DJ nights at weekends, and it serves snacks, pizza and salads, plus Sunday brunch until 3pm.

(8) Small
Aristotelous 10

Artwork depicting famous fairy-tale characters cover the walls of this café. It opens into the evenings with occasional live music.

(9) Adonis
Alexandrou Papanastasiou 57, Kastella

Located in Kastella, the most picturesque neighbourhood in Piraeus, Adonis serves snacks, fruit juices and coffee in the morning, and excellent food for lunch and dinner.

(10) Troubar
Filonos 131, Piraeus

Run by five friends who studied film together, Troubar stages weekend concerts – soul, funk, rock and jazz – with free admission. The long wooden bar and warm red lighting create a cosy atmosphere, reminiscent of an old-fashioned cabaret club.

See map on pp108–9

🔟 North to Delphi

The landscape changes as soon as you reach Athens' northern suburbs; the sight of pine-clad Mount Parnitha opens the way to the varied landscape of central Greece. The region, Sterea Ellada, is fringed with mountains, lined with coastal towns and dotted with Byzantine monasteries and ancient ruins. Delphi is the country's most beautiful Classical site. Here, the fabled Oracle voiced its prophecies, telling Oedipus, among others, of his terrible fate. Delphi's surrounds are full of opportunities for swimming, museum-touring and skiing.

Picturesque coastal town of Galaxidi

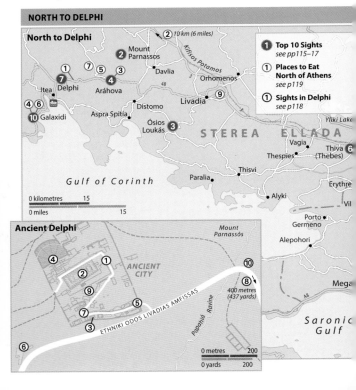

NORTH TO DELPHI

❶	**Top 10 Sights** *see pp115–17*
①	**Places to Eat North of Athens** *see p119*
①	**Sights in Delphi** *see p118*

Ancient temple ruins in Eleusis

1 Ancient Eleusis
MAP S2 ■ 210 554 6019
■ Bus 876 from Egaleo metro station
■ Open 8am–8pm daily (until 3pm during winter) ■ Adm

For 1,400 years, this was one of Greece's most sacred places. Thousands of pilgrims took part in the Eleusian Mysteries, rites that celebrated Demeter, goddess of nature, and her daughter Persephone. Modern Elefsina is a depressed industrial town and a surprising European Co-Capital of Culture in 2021. There are still some scattered ruins, and an archaeological museum, which is open during the same hours, to help make sense of them.

2 Mount Parnassos
MAP R1 ■ Parnassos Ski Centre
■ www.onparnassos.gr/en

Although developed in parts, Mount Parnassos offers splendid views, fine skiing and, in spring, wonderful trekking over wildflower-covered heights. The highest peak and most popular trek is at 2,457m (8,061 ft) on Liakoura. The truly ambitious can trek via Delphi by starting from Arahova very early in the morning, although this requires a large-scale hiking map. The best commercial product is Anavasi Edition's 1:35,000 Topo 2.1 'Mt Parnassos', most reliably sourced from their Athens shop at Voulis 32, Syndagma.

3 Osios Loukas
MAP R1 ■ 10am–5pm daily
■ Adm

This is a contender for the most beautiful monastery in Greece, with its idyllic location, looking across a valley to the soaring Elikonas mountain range. The main church, built in 1040, conceals glorious mosaics on the domed ceiling. The crypt has vivid post-Byzantine frescoes.

Ceiling frescoes, Osios Loukas

The mountain village of Arahova

4 Arahova
MAP R1 ■ Several buses daily from Terminal B, stopping en route to Delphi

This mountain village makes a good base for visiting Delphi and Parnassos. It is a popular winter destination for trendy Athenians, and room prices are higher here in winter. Though the main thoroughfare is lined with shops hawking local wine, noodles and cheese, the best way to explore is to get lost in its stone-lined passageways.

5 Evvia
MAP T1 ■ Halkida tourist office: www.dimoschalkideon.gr/en ■ Train times and prices: www.trainose.gr/en

Greece's second-largest island is so close to the mainland that you can reach it by bridge. There are up to eight trains a day from Larissa station in Athens to Halkida, Evvia's central city. The spine of mountains running north to south and dotted with villages offers great weekend trekking, and if you go by car mid-week you'll likely have its beaches and the thermal spas at the northern tip to yourself.

6 Thiva (Thebes)
MAP S2 ■ Buses hourly from Terminal B ■ Museum: Open May–Oct: 8am–8pm Tue–Sun (Nov–Apr: until 3pm) ■ Adm

This city was once one of the greatest Mycenaean settlements and home of the tragic dynasty of Oedipus. Next to nothing remains of the ancient sites, and the modern city offers little in the way of sightseeing, but the town's archaeological museum, re-opened in 2017 after extensive refurbishment, is worth a visit. It houses artifacts such as the Tanagra figurines.

7 Delphi
This was considered the centre of the world, as Zeus divined by releasing two eagles from opposite ends of the universe and seeing where they met. Great mystic powers are associated with this site, whose jutting mountain, gaping chasms and rushing springs indicate a place of dramatic geological upheaval. In ancient times, the Pythian priestess presided over the Oracle of Delphi, which gave famously abstruse prophecies. Apollo won dominion over the Oracle by defeating the serpent Python, and Apollo's temple is the focus of the site (see p120).

Temple of Apollo ruins, Delphi

ORACLE OF DELPHI

The Oracle delivered divine prophecies through a priestess at the Sanctuary of Apollo. The priestess practised consciousness-altering rituals, which probably included chewing laurel leaves and poppies and inhaling the vapours rising from a natural chasm where Python had been imprisoned. She communicated the prophecies in a series of inarticulate cries, which priests translated into verse.

→ *See map on pp114–15*

Byzantine art in Dafni monastery

8 Dafni
MAP T2 ■ 210 581 1558 ■ Bus 866 from Metro Agia Marina towards Aspropyrgos (30-minute journey) ■ Open 8am–3pm Tue & Fri

The lovely, domed, 11th-century monastic church here, decorated with brilliant mosaics, is one of the greatest treasures of Byzantine art.

9 Mount Parnitha
MAP T2

This beautiful mountain on the outskirts of Athens has many walking paths lined with pine and fir forests, which have reduced since the 2007 fire. In spring, its meadows are full of wild flowers. There are two refuges for climbers and a large casino-cum-alpine hotel, reached by cable car from the suburb of Thrakomakedones, the usual starting point for walks.

10 Galaxidi
MAP Q1 ■ Three buses daily from Terminal B

This chic, low-key resort on the Gulf of Corinth makes a great base for visiting Delphi. Located between turquoise waters and green mountains, it is tranquil and idyllic, except on summer weekends, when Athenians pack the inns and tavernas. Otherwise, take the time to explore small museums and 19th-century mansions.

A DRIVING TRIP FROM ATHENS TO DELPHI

▶ DAY ONE

Set out from Athens, breaking up the three-hour drive to Delphi with stops at the monasteries of **Dafni** and **Osios Loukas** (see p115).

Close to Delphi, stay either at the seaside town of **Galaxidi**, if it's summer, or in the mountain village of **Arahova** in winter. If the former, check into the charming **Hotel Ganimede** (see p149) and spend the afternoon at the beach; if the latter, consider a family chalet at the **Elatos Resort & Health Club** (see p148). Here, you can take the afternoon to ski at the Parnassos Ski Centre, or to explore the many mountain trails.

DAY TWO

The next day, head to the ancient site of **Delphi** bright and early. Wander around the **Temple of Apollo**, considering the strange rituals of the ancient priestesses who delivered the Oracle's prnouncements. Be sure not to miss the **museum** or the nearby **Sanctuary of Athena Pronaia** (see p118).

If you are in a hurry to return to Athens, grab a snack at the taverna **Ta Skalakia** (p119) in Delphi. If not, try the feta in filo pastry with honey at **O Bebelis** in Galaxidi, or the sausages and grilled formaella cheese at Arahova's **Karaouli** (see p119).

Sanctuary of Athena Pronaia

Sights in Delphi

1 Sacred Way
This road retraces the route Apollo first followed to Delphi and ends at the temple dedicated to him. The view, of Mount Parnassos looming above and the plunging gorge below, is suitably humbling.

2 Temple of Apollo
This temple contained the *omphalos* (navel-stone), marking the centre of the world, as well as the Oracle. Most ancient authors mention how rulers from all over the world sent envoys with lavish offerings to hear the Oracle's prophecies.

3 Sifnian Treasury
This temple-like marble structure, built by envoys from Sifnos, was the richest and most beautiful of several similar treasuries, all built as offerings to the Oracle. Its statues are now displayed in the museum.

4 Theatre
Built in the 4th century BC, this is one of the best-preserved theatres of ancient Greece. It offers a sweeping view of the whole site, especially the dramatically varied landscape that makes Delphi sacred.

5 Roman Agora
This marketplace area was lined with stalls selling sacred objects, where visitors could buy offerings to the Oracle.

6 Delphi Museum
2265 082 312 ■ Museum: open summer: 10am–5pm Mon, 8am–8pm tue–Sun; winter: 8am–3pm daily ■ Site: open summer 8am–8pm daily (until 3pm in winter & public holidays ■ Adm
The museum houses the greatest offerings brought to the Oracle from around the world.

Athenian Treasury

7 Athenian Treasury
The Athenians decorated their offering with elegant friezes depicting their hometown heroes Theseus and Herakles. The latter's famous Twelve Labours were performed at the Oracle's behest.

8 Sanctuary of Athena Pronaia
The sanctuary to warrior-goddess Athena was believed to protect the Sanctuary of Apollo from invaders. Though many of the buildings have been destroyed, the enigmatic and round Tholos is the quintessential image of Delphi.

9 Sanctuary of the Earth Goddess
This rock circle around an opening in the earth celebrated the earliest deity associated with the Delphic Oracle: the earth goddess Gaia. The tradition of the Oracle and priestesses continued, under the later deity Apollo.

10 Castalian Spring
Though now mostly dry, this spring was where pilgrims purified themselves before entering the holy site. The elaborate fountain-house built around it is still visible.

Delphi Museum exhibit

Places to Eat North of Athens

PRICE CATEGORIES
For a three-course meal for one with half
a bottle of wine (or equivalent meal),
taxes and extra charges.

€ under €40   €€ €40–€60   €€€ over €60

1 Ta Skalakia
MAP Q1 ■ Ilia Sengouni,
modern Delfi ■ 6944 207 532 ■ €

Located on a stepped lane between
the two main roads, this friendly
place serves grilled local meat as
well as more elaborate dishes.

2 Gargandouas
MAP Q1 ■ V. Pavlou, Delfi
village ■ €

A favourite among both locals
and visitors, this place is a
carnivore heaven.

3 Kaplanis
MAP R1 ■ Platía Tropeon,
Arahova ■ 2267 031 891 ■ €

Flavourful meaty classics served
in a room with gilded chandeliers. In
spring or fall, try the fried courgette
(zucchini) flowers. Year round, sample
the excellent house wine.

4 Albatross
MAP Q1 ■ Konstandinou Satha
36, Galaxidi ■ 2265 042 223 ■ €

This inland spot exels in dishes
such as rabbit or rooster stew
accompanied by great house wine.

5 Karaouli
MAP R1 ■ Kalyvia Livadi, 7 km
(4 miles) from Arahova ■ 2267 031
001 ■ Sep–Jun: Fri–Sun ■ €

A simple, traditional and delicious
taverna. Try the homemade spicy
Arahova sausage and stuffed peppers.

6 O Bebelis
MAP Q1 ■ Nikolaou Mama
20–22, Galaxidi ■ 2265 041 677 ■ €

Family-run O Bebelis serves Greek
dishes such as caramelized stuffed
onions, and pork with peppers in a
cosy setting with an open fireplace.

7 Babis
MAP R1 ■ Kalyvia Livadi,
Arachova ■ 2267 032 155 ■ Open for
lunch Oct–Apr daily and for dinner at
weekends ■ €

Go for a bowl of hot, aromatic *stifado*
stew *(see p64)*, as the crackling fire
casts a warm glow over everything.

8 Lykos Winery Restaurant
MAP T1 ■ Malakonta, west of
Eretria, Evvia ■ 222 906 8400 ■ €€

Expect traditional Greek meat and
fish dishes and fresh salads, plus
excellent wines. Lykos also runs
tours and tastings.

Elegant interiors of Taverna Nondas

9 Taverna Nondas
MAP R1 ■ 2 km (1.5 miles) from
Livadia ■ 2261 025 422 ■ €

Just outside Livadia, with ample
seating both indoors and out, Nondas
specializes in roast meats – charcoal-
grilled lamb chops, home-made
burgers and tender steak – accompanied by colourful salads. Generous
portions. It is closed on most Mondays.

10 Apanemo
MAP T1 ■ Ethnikis Symfiliosis
78, Halkida, Evvia ■ 2221 022 614 ■ €

Halkida is well-known for its
seafood *mezedopolia* which line
the waterfront. Apanemo is perfectly
set northeast of the pedestrian bridge.
It serves all the seafood standards
as well as local specialities such as
petrosolines (razor clams).

See map on pp114–15

🔟 Into the Peloponnese

Outside Athens, the Peloponnese is the part of Greece most steeped in myth and history. The Mycenaean kingdoms of Homer's *Iliad* were once believed to be merely legendary, until 19th-century German archaeologist Heinrich Schliemann unearthed their fabulous palaces on the Argive Peninsula. Now these sites compete with those in Athens as the most important in Greece. But, unlike Athens, the landscapes of those legends – the plains, where, according to Homer, great armies assembled, and the fields of Nemea where Herakles wrestled a lion to death – have remained mostly unchanged for millennia, making this one of the most beautiful regions of Greece, as well as the most fascinating.

Statue, Ancient Corinth

THE PELOPONNESE

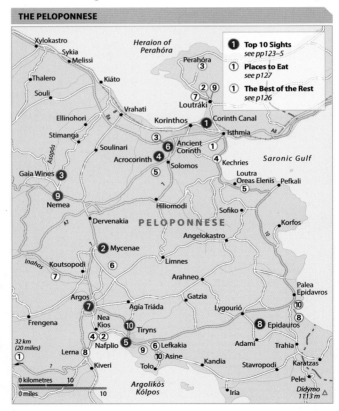

①	**Top 10 Sights** see pp123–5
①	**Places to Eat** see p127
①	**The Best of the Rest** see p126

Previous pages A yacht sailing through the Corinth Canal

Ferries sailing in the Corinth Canal

① Corinth Canal
MAP R3

The isthmus connecting mainland Greece to the Peloponnese frustrated sailors for thousands of years, forcing them to make long, dangerous journeys around the peninsula. Roman emperors Nero and Caligula tried digging a canal, but success came only in 1893, after French engineers had dynamited their way through the rock for 11 years. Boats take about an hour to make the 6-km (4-mile) journey. The bridge over the canal is popular with bungy-jumpers.

② Mycenae (Mykines)
MAP R3 ▪ Open Apr–Oct: 8am–6pm daily (Nov–Feb: until 3pm; Mar: until 5pm) ▪ Adm

Legend and history combine alluringly at Mycenae. Homer wrote of Greece's most powerful king during the Trojan War, Agamemnon, commanding the citadel of "well-built Mycenae, rich in gold." History confirms that there was indeed a Trojan War and a powerful civilization in Mycenae. Heinrich Schliemann discovered the palace at Mycenae in 1874, much of which accords with Homer's descriptions, including the wealth of gold.

③ Gaia Wines
MAP R3 ▪ Koutsi ▪ 2746 022 057 ▪ www.gaia-wines.gr ▪ Call or book online; book three weeks ahead for a tour and tasting during summer

The Greek wine industry has gained international acclaim by bringing serious cultivation techniques to its sun-drenched soils and indigenous grapes. Gaia is one of the best vineyards, producing deep velvety wines from Nemea's Agiogiorgitiko red and some white grapes.

④ Acrocorinth (Akrokorinthos)
MAP R3 ▪ Open winter: 8am–3pm daily (summer: may open later)

This towering rock outside Corinth was the strongest natural fortification in ancient Greece. In Archaic times it was crowned by a famous temple to Aphrodite. The structures you see today are mostly medieval Ottoman, often having been built over much older buildings. It is a strenuous hike to the top, but the effort is rewarded with 360 degree views.

The rock of Acrocorinth

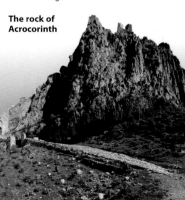

Colourful side street, Nafplio

5 Nafplio
**MAP R3 ■ Tourist office:
Martiou 25 ■ 2752 024 444**
Small, seaside Nafplio is one of
Greece's most beautiful towns. For
years the Ottomans and Venetians
fought for the city, leaving behind two
hilltop Venetian fortresses and several
mosques. The Greeks seized Nafplio
early in the independence war and
made it their first capital in 1829,
before Athens took that mantle.

6 Ancient Corinth
**MAP R3 ■ Archaeological sites:
Open summer: 8am–8pm daily (earlier
closure in Oct); winter: 8am–3pm Tue–
Sun ■ Adm**
Corinth's location, between the
Peloponnese and mainland Greece,
made it a rich and powerful trading

centre from Mycenaean times onwards.
Material wealth came with a reputation for wild and licentious lifestyles,
including polygamy and orgiastic cults,
which St Paul addressed with great
concern in the Bible (Epistle to the
Corinthians). After the 19th century,
Corinth declined into an unattractive
city. Its appeal resides in the remains
of the ancient glories, especially the
6th-century BC Temple of Apollo,
and the superb on-site museum.

7 Argos
**MAP R3 ■ Ancient theatre:
Open 8:30am–3pm Tue–Sun ■ Adm**
Believed to be the longest continually
inhabited town in Greece, the modern
town sits on top of the ancient one,
leaving much to wonder about but little
to see. The 4th-century theatre and
museum are well worth visiting once
they reopen after refurbishment; if you
have a car, drive up the Aspis hill, to the
medieval castle of Larissa overlooking
the plain immortalized by Homer.

THE LABOURS OF HERAKLES

Herakles was the son of Zeus and the
mortal Alkmene. Hera, enraged at her
husband Zeus's infidelity, drove Herakles
mad, causing him to kill his family. In
penance, he was required to perform
12 feats of heroism, out of which six of
them around the Peloponnese. He was
cleansed of his sin and glorified for his
feats, which, ironically, are attributed
to the jealous goddess: his name
means "glory of Hera".

The Temple of Apollo in Ancient Corinth, with Acrocorinth in background

8 Epidauros
MAP S3 ▪ Open May–Aug: 8am–8pm daily (Apr & Sep: until 7pm; Oct–Feb: until 5pm; Mar: until 6pm) ▪ Adm

The 4th-century BC Theatre of Epidauros is one of the best sites in Greece, marvellously preserved and with astounding acoustics *(see p72)*. Outside the theatre is the restored Asklepion, an ancient sanctuary devoted to Asklepios, the god of health.

Theatre of Epidauros

9 Nemea
MAP R3 ▪ Open May–Aug: 8am–8pm daily (Sep–Apr: until 5pm; mid-winter: until 3pm) ▪ Adm

This was the site of the first labour of Herakles: the slaying of the Nemean lion. The lion's skin was impenetrable, so Herakles strangled the beast, skinned it with its own claws and kept its pelt as a coat of armour. This is one of several legends connected with the founding of the Nemean Games (part of the Panhellenic Games). The highlight of Nemea is the temple of Zeus, with nine columns and two architraves that have been reconstructed.

10 Tiryns
MAP R3 ▪ Open May–Aug: 8am–8pm daily (Apr & Sep: until 7pm; Oct: until 6pm; May: until 6pm; Nov–Mar: until 3pm) ▪ Adm

One of the most important cities of the Mycenaean civilization, its fortifications of limestone were so massive that later Greeks believed they could have been built by the giant Kyklopes. Although not as grand as Mycenae, Tiryns has intriguing details on its walls.

OVERNIGHT IN NAFPLIO

▶ DAYTIME

Visit **Nafplio** on a summer weekend, buying tickets for a performance at Epidauros before setting off *(see p43)*.

Take a morning bus from Athens' Terminal A, having also booked a hotel in advance. The nicest place to stay is Nafplia Palace; Hotel Byron is more affordable but still good.

Spend the day exploring Nafplio's Old City. Buy some drinks and a snack, and take them up to the **Venetian fortress**, which affords glorious views of Nafplio and the Gulf of Argos. If you're feeling fit, climb the 999 steps to the top; otherwise, take a taxi.

Below the fortress, cool off at the small public beach. For more privacy, head down the walkway and go diving from the rocks.

NIGHTTIME

Dine at Aiolos Tavern *(see p127)*, returning to the bus station before 7:30pm, when buses depart for **Epidauros**. Even if the performance is in Greek, the powerful acting and magical setting will captivate. Programmes summarize the plot in English. Take the bus back to Nafplio and the hotel.

The following morning, check out, but leave your luggage at the hotel. Take an early bus to **Mycenae** *(see p123)*, whose tragic former inhabitants may well have been the subject of the previous night's play. Marvel at this legendary prehistoric city for a few hours, then go back to Nafplio and hop on a bus back to Athens.

See map on p122

The Best of the Rest

1 Isthmia
MAP R3 ▪ 2741 037 244
▪ 8:30am–3pm Tue–Sun ▪ Adm

Much of the ancient site has been destroyed, but mosaics of marine creatures remain. Here visitors can enjoy the vibrant 4th-century AD opus sectile panels portraying harbour scenes, bird-life and sea creatures.

2 Loutraki
MAP R2 ▪ Hydrotherapeutic Thermal Spa: Georgiou Lekka 24
▪ www.loutrakispa.gr

A popular weekend destination, Loutraki is known for its spring waters and its Hydrotherapeutic Thermal Spa. The area is also home to a casino that's said to be one of the biggest in Europe.

3 Heraion of Perahora
MAP R2 ▪ 8am–3pm daily

Though little remains here other than a Temple of Hera and a stoa, this is still an idyllic place to swim, with the wonderful Melangavi lighthouse, and crystal-clear waters. Snorkellers can see ancient ruins underwater.

Beach shore and sanctuary at Perahora

4 Kekhries
MAP R3

The site where Theseus defeated Sinis, the bandit who used whole pine trees to sling-shot victims across the water. Today the seaside town makes a nice stop on the drive to Epidauros.

5 Loutra Oreas Elenis
MAP R3

A perfect lunch stop en route from Athens to Epidauros, this seaside village offers swimming and is dotted with choice tavernas. According to legend, Helen of Troy once bathed in the small, warm spring here.

6 Heraion of Argos
MAP R3 ▪ N of Nafplio
▪ 8am–3pm

This sanctuary to goddess Hera, built between the 8th and 4th centuries BC, occupies three raised terraces, with great views over the Argive plain.

7 Skouras Wines
MAP R3 ▪ on Argos–Nemea road, nr Synora village ▪ www.skouras.gr

Skouras is known for its range of quality white, red and the rare (in Greece) rosé wines. Book ahead online to arrange a tour and tasting.

8 Lerna
MAP R4 ▪ 8am–3pm daily ▪ Adm

One of the oldest archaeological sites in Greece, with remains dating back to 2500 BC.

9 Agia Moni
MAP R3 ▪ Nr Nafplio

This 12th-century Byzantine convent and garden is worth a short stop en route to Epidavros.

10 Asine
MAP R4

This deserted Bronze Age settlement is set near a beach. Stop to admire the fortifications by the road. Nobel Laureate George Seferis paid homage to this place in his poem *The King of Asine*.

Places to Eat

1 Omorfo Tavernaki
MAP R3 ■ Vasilissis Olgas 1, Nafplio ■ 2752 025 944 ■ €

With a romantic interior, this taverna offers traditional greek dishes. It gets crowded during the Epidauros festival, so book in advance.

2 Stavlos Thrakotaverna
MAP R3 ■ Profiti Ilia 12, Nafplio ■ 2752 306 702 ■ €

Situated in the new town, this taverna offers lamb dishes as well as *kokoretsi* (offal on a spit). Meat-lovers would enjoy feasting here.

Marinos traditional taverna

3 Marinos
MAP R3 ■ Arhea Korinthos village ■ 2741 031 130 ■ €

Close to an archaeological site, Marinos is set in the village square. Try the *moussakas* (layers of meat and eggplant), grilled lamb chops, and salads.

4 Aiolos Tavern
MAP R3 ■ Vasilissis Olgas 30 ■ 2752 026 828 ■ €

Set in the heart of Nafplio, this cheerful family-run taverna offers traditional fare, from slow-cooked beans and grilled meats to cabbage rolls.

5 To Pefko
MAP R3 ■ Loutra Oreas Elenis ■ 2741 033 801 ■ €

With outdoor seating, this restaurant offers tasty squid and sand smelt, as well as plenty of vegetarian options, paired with rosé wine. Take a quick dip until your order arrives.

PRICE CATEGORIES
For a three-course meal for one with half a bottle of wine (or equivalent meal), taxes and extra charges.

€ under €40   €€ €40–€60   €€€ over €60

6 Psalidas
MAP R3 ■ Lefkakia, 7 km (4 miles) E of Nafplio ■ 2752 061 814 ■ €

In the sleepy village of Lefkakia, Psalidas serves authentic home cooking in a pretty garden. Expect meaty stews, seasonal vegetables such as artichokes in spring and peppers in summer, and excellent local red wine. Book ahead on weekends.

7 Paleo Diporto
MAP R2 ■ Konstandinou Boleti 9, Loutraki ■ 2744 300 852 ■ €

A genuine mezeopolio, this place is set away from the shore esplanade. Enjoy the traditional live music with locals here on weekends during the evenings. It remains closed between May and September.

8 Kalogerikon
MAP R3 ■ Palea Epidavros ■ 2753 042 090 ■ €

Housed in a stone-built coastal resort, this restaurant has an inviting garden and orange grove. Enjoy seasonal meat dishes and *moussakas* with wine.

9 Rigani
MAP R2 ■ Papanikolaou 5, Loutraki ■ 2744 066 744 ■ €

With its innovative approach to traditional recipes, Rigani offers high-quality taverna food. Enjoy it in the cool garden, framed and shaded by trees and vineyards.

10 Mouria Restaurant - Gikas Holidays Club
MAP S3 ■ Palea Epidavros, Argolida ■ 2753 041 218 ■ €

The food here is rooted firmly in the Greek tradition: fresh locally caught fish, fine grilled meats and delicious home-made desserts.

See map on p122

🔟 Around the Attica Coast

From as early as the 5th century BC, the ancients built marble temples to their gods on verdant slopes covered in the dense foliage

of dark pines. This is a land where the legendary Theseus once roamed, freeing Attica from a scourge of monsters. Crowning the peninsula, at southernmost Cape Sounio, was the stunning Temple of Poseidon, sparkling like a beacon over the Aegean. Looking at Attica today, it is clear to see that parts of the coast have fallen victim to overdevelopment, but the jewels of Attica remain in the peacefully crumbling temples among the trees, in the best of the region's sandy beaches and in the ultra-luxurious summer clubs, which stretch down the coast as far as Varkiza.

Sanctuary of Artemis, Vravrona

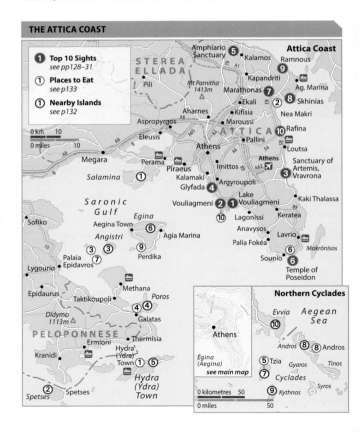

THE ATTICA COAST

- ① **Top 10 Sights** *see pp128–31*
- ① **Places to Eat** *see p133*
- ① **Nearby Islands** *see p132*

The picturesque thermal Lake Vouliagmeni, offering year-round bathing

1 Lake Vouliagmeni
MAP T3 ▪ Bus 122 from Metro Elliniko ▪ Open summer: 7:30am–8pm ▪ Adm ▪ www.limnivouliagmenis.gr
Bathers come year-round to take the warm, therapeutic waters of Lake Vouliagmeni, a large thermal spring that maintains a steady temperature of 22–25 °C (72–77 °F). The source of the clear, half-fresh, half-salt waters is still unknown, but devotees say there's no doubt about their healing properties. It's a great place to swim, especially on cold winter mornings, flanked by a high rock face on one side and trees on the other.

2 Vouliagmeni
MAP T3 ▪ Bus E22 from Athens
A sprawling seaside resort suburb south of Athens, Vouliagmeni is fringed with luxury hotels, yacht clubs and pricey pay-per-visit beaches. But the biggest draw for Athenians and visitors are the super-glam beachside clubs, the centre of nightlife in summer. All are re-created in luscious over-the-top decor each year.

3 Sanctuary of Artemis, Vravrona
MAP T3 ▪ Markopoulo, Mesogia ▪ Open 8am–3pm Tue–Sun ▪ Adm
This temple to Artemis, goddess of the hunt and childbirth, was once the most sacred in Attica. Its highlight was the Arkteia festival, where young girls dressed as cubs performed the "bear dance" in honour of the goddess's favourite animal. When King Agamemnon sacrificed his daughter Iphigenia to Artemis, the goddess saved her and brought her here, where she became a high priestess. Her tomb is the oldest cult shrine on the site. The tranquil site is complete with a colonnade and a sacred spring. It also offers an excellent museum that was refurbished in 2009.

Shopping in Glyfada

4 Glyfada
MAP T3 ▪ Bus 124 from metro Elliniko, or Tram from Syndagma
Here, a wealthy, if somewhat overdeveloped beach-resort and flashy nightlife vibe prevail. There are plenty of designer shops and cafés to sit in while sporting new purchases by day, and trendy summer clubs to dance in by night.

Ruins at the Amphiario Sanctuary

THE LOCAL HERO

Theseus is linked with Attica through a mix of mythology and enticing traces of historical evidence that suggest that a King Theseus may have actually existed. This king managed to unite the region's splinter states, while the reputation of Theseus the hero rests on tales of his slaying monsters and bedding everyone from Helen of Troy to Hippolyta, Queen of the Amazons.

5 Amphiario Sanctuary

MAP T2 ■ Open 8am–3pm ■ Adm

Dedicated in the late 5th century BC, this shrine was an oracle and a health resort. It honoured Amphiaraos, King of Argos, tricked into fighting against Thebes, even though he foresaw that he would be killed. Zeus arranged for the earth to swallow him on the battlefield, and be reincarnated as a demi-god. There is a small theatre complete with stage and a stoa.

6 Temple of Poseidon

MAP T3 ■ 2292 039 363 ■ Bus from Mavromateon terminal in Athens (2-hour journey time) ■ Open summer & winter: 9am–sunset daily ■ Adm

The 5th-century BC temple is one of the few ever built to Poseidon. After

Temple of Poseidon on Cape Sounio

watching the sunset from the white marble pillars of this ancient site on the peak of Cape Sounio, you may share the sentiments of the poet Byron. He asked the gods simply to "Place me on Sunium's marbled steep, Where nothing save the waves and I, May hear our mutual murmurs sweep, There, swanlike, let me sing and die." *(See also p53.)*

7 Marathon (Marathonas)

MAP T2 ■ Marathon tomb: 2294 055 462 ■ Museum: 2294 055 155 ■ Open 8am–3pm Tue–Sun (for both all year round) ■ Buses daily from Mavromateon terminal ■ Adm (for both)

In 490 BC, the Marathon plain was the site of one of history's most important battles. There, an army of 10,000 Greeks defeated 25,000 Persians, preserving the newly founded first democracy. A tomb to the 192 Greek soldiers who fell (in comparison to 6,000 Persians) still stands here. After the victory, Pheidippides ran the 42 km (26 miles) to Athens to announce the outcome, then collapsed dead on the spot. A museum displays finds from the area.

8 Skhinias
MAP T2 ■ KTEL bus from the Mavromateon terminal

Many consider Skhinias the most beautiful beach area in Attica, its white-sand coast hugged by dark pine forests. An giant rowing course was constructed on the wetlands for the 2004 Olympics, despite this being an environmentally protected area. Several rustic, illegal tavernas at the beach have been demolished. However, visitors can lunch at the nearby Marathonas beach.

9 Ramnous (Ramnounda)
MAP T2 ■ Open 8am–3pm Tue–Sun ■ Adm

The 5th-century ruins of these temples to Nemesis (goddess of divine retribution) and Themis (goddess justice and law) are among Greece's most unspoiled sites. There is an ancient fortress situated just adjacent, which defended the important harbour.

Temple ruins at Ramnous

10 Rafina
MAP T2 ■ KTEL bus from the terminal on Mavromateon

If you go to the islands of Andros or Evvia, you'll spend time in Rafina, Attica's third port along with Piraeus and Lavrio. It's smaller and cleaner than chaotic Piraeus, but still bustling, filled with quayside seafood tavernas as well as the traffic of embarking and disembarking ferries. The environs of Rafina were devastated by a firestorm in July 2018, and so the local beaches have lost their appeal due to the utterly blackened backdrop.

A TOUR OF ATTICA

▶ MORNING

Start early with a drive out of Athens to **Marathonas**. Survey the plain where the Greeks won history's greatest military victory, and pay homage at the warrior's tomb. Then head to the ruins of **Ramnous**, focusing more on the scenery than the site's original purpose: praying for revenge.

Drive south down the coast, to the **Sanctuary of Artemis** at Vravona and its fine museum *(see p129)*, which closes at 3pm. Then have lunch in nearby Loutsa, at **To Korali** *(Vravronos 62 • 2294 045 044 • open all day from noon)*

AFTERNOON

Head to one of Greece's most splendid sights: the **Temple of Poseidon** at Sounio. If it's still daylight, go to one of the two nearby beaches. The one to the east of the temple access lane requires an athletic scramble down but offers scenic seclusion; the hotel beach to the northwest is more accessible but covered with sun loungers. An hour before sunset, wander up to the temple, and watch as the marble columns turn to pink and gold.

Returning to the coastal drive to Athens, consider two dinner options. The nearby taverna **Syrtaki**, back towards Lavrio, or, closer to the city, Nobu's **Matsuhisa Athens** in Vouliagmeni, *(see p133)* where you can end your day with exquisite Japanese fusion cuisine and a romantic view of the Aegean Sea below a starlit sky.

See map on p128 ←

Nearby Islands

1 Salamina (Salamis)
MAP S3

Ancient Salamis had a rich history. Playwright Euripides was born here, and in 480 BC, the Greeks famously beat Xerxes off the shore. Visit the Faneromeni convent for its frescoes as well as the clean south coast beaches.

2 Spetses
MAP S4

Popular with British tourists, Spetses offers pine forests, good beaches and a charming harbour town. Automobiles are restricted in town, but allowed along the island ring road.

3 Angistri
MAP S3

This tiny hispter islet off Egina has several beaches, clear beautiful water, a handful of small hotels and tavernas, and not much else.

4 Poros
MAP S4

Volcanic Poros comprises two joined islands, Sferia and Kalavria. The town of Sferia is worth a visit, and Kalavria has pine trees, beaches as well as the Zoödohou Pigis monastery.

5 Hydra (Ydra)
MAP S4

Lovely Hydra town, its marble-paved lanes winding among the old mansions around the busy harbour, is one of Greece's most beautiful spots. Its popularity as a celebrity getaway hasn't dented its charm.

Seafront at Hydra

6 Egina
MAP S3

An easy and rewarding day trip, only 45 minutes from Athens, with an atmospheric town, famously tasty pistachios, the Temple of Aphaia, and the ghost village of Paleohora, with several frescoed chapels.

Temple of Aphaia at Egina

7 Kea (Tzia)
MAP U3

Although only an hour by ferry from Lavrio, Kea is peaceful and away from the port, and its interior is covered by oak trees. Don't miss the Archaic Lion of Kea, carved into a hillside.

8 Andros
MAP V3

A favourite of Greece's weathy, golden-beached Andros is exclusive and hiker-friendly. The Goulandris Museum of Contemporary Art holds exhibits every summer, complementing the permanent collection.

9 Kythnos
MAP U4

Mostly barren and less picturesque than the other Cyclades, Kythnos boasts thermal springs at Loutra and great beaches.

10 Evvia
MAP S1–U2

Only the southern part of Evvia is easily visited from Athens. The main attractions here are the Neo-Classical town of Karystos, nearby beaches and the hiking trails on Mount Ohi.

Places to Eat

PRICE CATEGORIES
For a three-course meal for one with half a bottle of wine (or equivalent meal), taxes and extra charges.

€ under €40   €€ €40–€60   €€€ over €60

① Gitoniko, Hydra
MAP S4 ▪ 2298 053 615 ▪ €

Both visitors and locals flock to this backstreet taverna with a roof-top seating. They serve *magirefta* along with decent bulk wine.

② O Psaras
MAP T2 ▪ Leoforos Poseidonos 3, Marathonas Beach ▪ 2294 055 237 ▪ €

Enjoy octopus, barbecued fresh fish and a Greek salad under canvas sunshades on a wooden deck on Marathon's sandy beach. Start with their exceptional *mezedes*.

③ Parnasssos
MAP T2 ▪ Metohi hamlet, Angistri islet ▪ 2297 091 339 ▪ €

Apart from standard grills and starters, this inland spot above the port serves its own cheese, a few daily *magirefta* and decent *hyma* wine.

④ Platanos
MAP T3 ▪ Platia Agiou Georgiou, Poros ▪ 2298 026 661 ▪ €

Set inland under a *platanos* (plane tree), this taverna serves meat grills as well as seafood. It also offers plenty of vegetarian options.

⑤ Patralis, Spetses
MAP S4 ▪ Kounoupitsa waterfront ▪ 2298 075 380 ▪ €

Specializing in seafood, this taverna offers fish in Spetsiota sauce and *astakomakaronada* (noodles with lobster flakes). Great terrace views.

⑥ Syrtaki, nr Sounio
MAP T3 ▪ 2 km (1 mile) N of Poseidon Temple, towards, Lavrio ▪ 2292 039 125 ▪ €€

The most popular taverna around Sounio. Eat seafood at the shaded three-storey seating area, which offers great views of the sea.

⑦ To Steki tis Ritsas, Kea
MAP U3 ▪ Ioulida village, towards Lion ▪ 2288 022 088 ▪ €

Skip the expensive tavernas at the port in favour of this traditional, family-run establishment serving local recipes.

⑧ Endochora, Andros
MAP V3 ▪ G. Embirikou, Andros Town ▪ 2282 023 207 ▪ €

In Andros' car-free Old Town, Endochora serves contemporary Mediterranean fare in a white-washed shabby-chic interior. Try a variety of cheese with candied grapes, grilled salmon with wild rice, and their signature cucumber salad with poppy seeds and chilli sauce.

Traditional Greek salad with feta cheese

⑨ Deka, Egina
MAP S3 ▪ Perdika waterfront ▪ 2297 061 231 ▪ €

Around since 1943, this is the oldest and most reliable taverna at the harbour. The menu includes exceptional and well-priced seafood.

⑩ Matsuhisa Athens, Vouliagmeni
MAP T3 ▪ Apollonos 40 ▪ 210 896 0510 ▪ €€€

At the Astir Palace Hotel, chef Nobu Matsuhisa presents his Japanese-Peruvian fusion cuisine. Seafood predominates, from his signature black cod with miso to sushi rolls and sashimi tacos. Smart ambience, with stunning views over the Aegean Sea.

See map on p128

Streetsmart

Evzones at the Changing of the Guard

Getting To and Around Athens

Arriving by Air

Athens International Airport lies 27 km (16.5 miles) southeast of the city centre, to which it is connected by various means of public transport. The metro (M3, blue) runs directly from the airport half hourly to Syndagma and Monastiraki, in the city centre. In addition, there are four 24-hour bus services: the X95 runs to Syndagma; the X96 to Piraeus port; the X93 to the KTEL Kifissos bus station; and the X97 to Elliniko metro station (M2, red). Taxis are also readily available; the journey takes about 40 minutes in light traffic and operates on a fixed tariff.

Aegean Airlines, the largest Greek airline, flies into Athens from most European capitals, including London, Edinburgh, Dublin, Paris, Rome, Berlin and Madrid, as well as from Russia and the Middle East. **British Airways, Ryanair, Jet2** and **easyJet** fly in from the UK, while **Delta** flies direct from New York (JFK) in the US, and **Air Canada** and **Air Transat** fly direct from several points in Canada.

Arriving by Train

Greek trains are run by **TrainOSE**. However, the national network is quite limited – partly due to the country's mountainous topography – therefore, Greeks prefer to travel by bus rather than by train. The main train line is from Thessaloniki in the north to Athens' Larissis train station in Kolonos, and is served by fast InterCity trains. International trains run every day from Sofia (Bulgaria), from Belgrade (Serbia) and also from Skopje (North Macedonia) to Thessaloniki.

Arriving by Road

Major roads connecting Greece to its neighbours run to Thessaloniki: the E90 from Turkey, the E79 from Bulgaria and the E75 from North Macedonia, which merge west of Thessaloníki as the E75/A1 on towards Athens (502 km/312 miles). To the west, Patras is connected to Athens (210 km/130.5 miles) by the A8. Drivers must pay at often closely spaced toll stations.

Long-distance coaches from all over Greece run to Athens, ending their journeys at either **KTEL Kifissos** (Bus Terminal A) or **KTEL Liosion** (Bus Terminal B), both north-west of the city centre.

Arriving by Sea

Athens is served by the port of Piraeus, the largest and busiest passenger port in Europe. Each day, many ferries, catamarans and hydrofoils arrive from the Greek islands, transporting both locals and visitors to the capital. Many cruise ships sailing around the eastern Mediterranean also dock at Piraeus.

For ferry timetables and booking, see the **Greek Ferries, GTP** or **Open Seas** websites, which cover every main company that has operations from the islands.

Travelling by Bus and Trolleybus

Buses and trolleybuses, cheap but often very crowded, are operated by **Athens Urban Transport Organization (OASA)**. Multi-coloured (largely purple) trolleybuses serve the city centre, while the blue-and-white buses run out to the city's suburbs.

Travelling by Metro and Tram

Urban Rail Transport SA (STASY) operates three metro lines: the M1 (green) running from Piraeus to Kifissia; the M2 (red) from Anthoupoli to Elliniko; and the M3 (blue) from Agia Marina to Doukissis Plakentias, with an extension to the airport. The main nodes are the stations at Syndagma, Monastiraki and Omonia.

The same company runs three tram lines in a triangular network that connects the city centre and the west Attica Coast. The lines run between Syndagma, the Stadium of Peace and Friendship (ΣΕΦ on electronic displays) at Neo Faliro and Asklipio Voulas (near the seaside suburb of Glyfada).

Buying Tickets and Travel Cards

Late in 2017, Athens' public transport ticket system switched to electronic smartcards (labelled ATH.ENA.

TICKET), easiest to buy at Metro stations; very few *peripteras* (streetcorner kiosks) will stock them. They are integrated to cover bus, trolleybus, tram and metro (but not routes to the airport). One ticket costs €1.40 and is valid for 90 minutes from the moment you stamp it at the beginning of your first journey; you can load many journeys onto one reusable card, and the price drops the more you add – eg €2.70 for two trips, €6.50 for five trips at any time. A day ticket costs €4.50 and a five-day ticket €9. For the airport, a single express bus ticket is €6 and a regular metro ticket is €10 (there are discounts for two or more passengers). A tourist ticket is available for €22 and includes a round trip to the airport, metro, tram and bus for three days. There are reductions on some fares for those over 65, kids and students.

Travelling by Car

Negotiating Athens by car can be intimidating. Traffic congestion and endless parking problems mean you are advised to do without a car during your time in the capital; you may want to hire a vehicle for trips to the many sights beyond Athens on the Greek mainland. Most companies have offices at the top of Syngrou, near the Zeus temple.

If you have a car, try to choose a hotel that guarantees parking. If this is not feasible, there are several big car parks close to the centre. Most are located next to metro stations, two of the biggest

being at Syngrou-Fix (Koukaki neighbourhood) and Kerameikos (Gazi neighbourhood) – though these are expensive and often crowded. Car break-ins are common, especially in Exárhia and Gazi, so leave no visible valuables wherever you park.

Travelling by Taxi

The yellow Athenian taxis are affordable, and most drivers are honest. It is common to hail a passing taxi in the street, but this can be difficult for foreigners, due to the language barrier and the notorious gruff attitude of Athenian taxi drivers. Visitors will probably find it easier to wait at a taxi rank (there's one on almost every city square) or to ask a hotel receptionist to call a taxi. It's also normal for a taxi to pick up additional passengers heading in a similar direction.

Travelling by Bicycle

For years, the idea of riding a bicycle in Athens sounded absurd, but since the onset of the economic crisis, more and more locals have bought bikes and started cycling around the city. However, there are no official bike lanes and car drivers still have a low tolerance, so take care while riding.

Travelling on Foot

Athens' city centre is a joy to walk around, and all the main sites can be reached on foot from Syndagma. There is a slowly increasing number of pedestrian-only

streets – pick your route carefully and you can avoid traffic altogether. The hilltops of the Acropolis and Lykavittos are often visible and can usefully be used as orientation points.

Practical Information

Passports and Visas

Visitors from the EU (plus Norway, Switzerland and Iceland) can freely enter Greece with an ID card or passport – but should register with the police after 90 days. Visitors from the US, Australia, Canada and New Zealand need only a valid passport for entry (no visa required) and can stay for up to 90 days, cumulative, in any 180-day period. For longer stays, they must obtain a resident's permit from the Alien's Bureau in Athens. Nationals from most of the other countries need a visa and should consult the **Hellenic Republic Ministry of Foreign Affairs** website or the Greek embassy in their country of origin. Schengen visas are valid for Greece.

Customs Regulations

EU citizens are no longer subjected to export limits on alcohol, tobacco and perfume for personal use. Import limits for EU citizens are: 800 cigarettes, 400 cigarillos, 200 cigars, 1 kg of smoking tobacco, 10 litres of spirits over 22 per cent, 20 litres of alcoholic beverages under 22 per cent, 90 litres of wine (60 litres of sparkling wine) and 110 litres of beer.

Visitors aged over 17 from non-EU countries can carry the following items in their personal luggage: 200 cigarettes or 250 g of smoking tobacco, 1 litre of spirits, 4 litres of still wine and 16 litres of beer. There are strict limits on the import and export of antiquities, archaeological artifacts, firearms and weapons.

Travel Safety Advice

Visitors can get up-to-date travel safety information from the **UK Foreign and Commonwealth Office**, the **US State Department** and the **Australian Department of Foreign Affairs and Trade**.

Travel Insurance

Travellers should get comprehensive travel insurance against theft or loss, accidents, illness, and travel delays or cancellations. Greece has a reciprocal health agreement with other EU countries, and EU visitors will receive emergency treatment if they carry a **European Health Insurance Card (EHIC)**. However, dental care is not covered. Non-EU visitors should check if their home country has reciprocal agreements with Greece before travelling.

Health

No vaccinations are required to visit Greece, health hazards are few, and the tap water in the city is of excellent quality. For minor ailments, visit a *farmakeio* (pharmacy). They are marked with a large green cross on a white background, and are open 8:30am–2pm Mon–Fri. They also have a rotation system for working in the afternoon, at night and on weekends. If your nearest pharmacy is closed, there will be a notice in the window – in both Greek and Latin alphabets – with the address of the next nearest pharmacy that will be on duty at that time.

Among the main public hospitals in Athens are **Evangelismos** in Kolonaki, in the city centre, and **Gennimatas** in Holargos, a short distance east of the centre. The **KAT Hospital** in Kifisia is designated for treating fractured bones and grave injuries. **Hygeia** in Marousi, north of the centre, is a big private hospital.

Since the onset of the economic crisis and the imposition of stringent austerity measures, public hospitals have been severely underfunded and understaffed. Corruption has always been rife in the Greek healthcare system, and many doctors expect "under-the-table" payments – the fabled *fakelaki* or envelope stuffed with cash – for priority treatment.

Personal Security

Despite press reports, Athens remains one of the safest capital cities in Europe. Big public demonstrations and protest marches may look alarming, especially when the police fire tear-gas at the crowds, but they are regarded as a normal part of Greek life. If demonstrations do turn violent, this normally happens at Syndagma Square, in front of the Parliament.

If you don't want to be involved, avoid this area on days when strikes and marches are announced.

Since the onset of the crisis, Athens' crime rate, especially pickpocketing, has risen. Organised gangs target airport buses arriving at Syndagma, and the cars and platforms of the Monastiraki Line M1 station. If you are heavily laden with bags, it may be a good idea for you to get off at the next stop and take a taxi back to your destination – it's cheaper than replacing wallets and their contents. Busy areas of the city are most often very safe at night. However, the neighbourhood around Omonia Square can be intimidating and is best avoided after dark, as it has become a magnet for drug addicts and people from marginalized communities, while Platia Viktorias, situated north of Omonia, has turned into an unofficial gathering point for refugees as well as immigrants.

If you have cause to complain about shops, restaurants, tour guides or taxi drivers, you should contact the **tourist police**. Their job is to resolve any problems that are related tourism, and they speak several foreign languages, including English. Thefts, though, should be rep... the police in c... precinct in wh... has occurred.

Emergency Services

The ambulance service, fire brigade and police can be reached on the **European Emergency Number**. In addition to this, there are dedicated lines for each of these emergency services. In the case of a medical emergency, another option that is available is **SOS Doctors**, a private organization on call 24/7, though be aware that its services are not covered under public healthcare.

DIRECTORY

PASSPORTS AND VISAS

Australia
MAP H2 ■ Level 6, Thon Building, Kifisias and Alexandras Avenue, Ambelokipi
📞 210 870 4000
🌐 greece.embassy.gov.au

Canada
Ethnikis Antistaseos 48, Halandri
📞 210 727 3400
🌐 canadainternational.gc.ca/greece-grece

Hellenic Republic Ministry of Foreign Affairs
🌐 mfa.gr

New Zealand (Consulate)
Kifissias 76, Ambelokipi
📞 210 692 4136

Republic of Ireland
MAP E5 ■ Vassileos Konstantinou 7
📞 210 723 2771
🌐 dfa.ie/irish-embassy/greece

United Kingdom
MAP F4 ■ Ploutarhou 1
📞 210 727 2600
🌐 gov.uk/government/world/organisations/british-embassy-athens

USA
MAP G3
■ Vasilissis Sofias 91
📞 210 721 2951
🌐 gr.usembassy.gov

TRAVEL SAFETY ADVICE

Australian Department of Foreign Affairs and Trade
🌐 dfat.gov.au
🌐 smartraveller.gov.au

UK Foreign and Commonwealth Office
🌐 gov.uk/foreign-travel-advice

US State Department
🌐 travel.state.gov

HEALTH

Evangelismos Hospital
Ypsilandou 45-47
📞 213 204 1000
🌐 evaggelismos-hosp.gr

Gennimatas Hospital
Mesogeion 154, Holargos, Metro Ethniki Amyna
📞 213 203 2000
🌐 gna-gennimatas.gr

Hygeia Hospital
Erthrou Stavrou 4 and Kifissias, Marousi
📞 210 686 7425
🌐 hygeia.gr

KAT Hospital
Nikis 2, Klfisia
📞 213 208 6000
🌐 kat-hosp.gr

PERSONAL SECURITY

Tourist police
📞 1571

EMERGENCY SERVICES

Ambulance
📞 166

European Emergency Number
📞 112

Fire
📞 199

Police
📞 100

SOS Doctors
📞 1016

Travellers with Specific Needs

Although there have been massive improvements here, Greece still has a long way to go in terms of catering for the needs of disabled travellers. Some of the main attractions, such as the Acropolis and the Acropolis Museum, offer wheelchair access, but in general facilities are limited. As of 2018, all hotels by law must provide at least one room with disabled access, though compliance often is spotty. Metro stations in Athens are equipped with lifts that are large enough for those using wheelchairs, and most blue-and-white buses have middle-door ramps for wheelchairs. Major crosswalks have the kerb scooped out, but pips for sight-impaired pedestrians are rare. Disabled visitors enjoy free entry to state-run archaeological sites and museums.

Organisations such as **Accessible Travel Greece** and **Sage Traveling** offer good help and advice for disabled travellers.

Currency and Banking

Greece is a member of the Eurozone and uses the euro (€), which is divided into 100 cents (*lepta* in Greek). Currency notes are available in denominations of €500, €200, €100, €50, €20, €10 and €5. Coins come in denominations of €2, €1 and 50, 20, 10, 5, 2 and 1 cents. It is best to not accept the three notes of the highest value, as they can be difficult to use in transactions.

ATMs (cash machines) are widely available and serve as the easiest way to get cash. Surcharges depend on your bank. Alternatively, foreign currencies can be exchanged for euros at bureaux de change in central Athens. A passport or ID card is required when currencies are being exchanged.

Credit and debit cards (Visa, American Express and MasterCard) are widely accepted; suprisingly, small establishments now have a card machine (*mihanima POS* in Greek). If your card is stolen, inform the police and your credit card company at once.

Internet and Telephone

Most of the restaurants, hotels and cafés in the city offer free Wi-Fi access. Syndagma Square, in the city centre offers a free Wi-Fi hotspot.

The dialling code for Greece is 0030, and the city codes for Athens are 210, 211, 212 and 213. Provincial codes in Attica, the mainland and the Peloponnese each have five digits. Fixed line as well as mobile numbers have 10 digits in total – dial all 10.

Most mobile phones will work in Greece and roaming charges have been scrapped in the EU with effect from June 2017. Visitors from outside the EU can buy a local SIM card that they can use in an unlocked mobile phone to avoid having to pay roaming charges. Both the phone and the SIM card must be registered upon purchase, as part of anti-terrorism measures.

Postal Services

The main branch of Greece's **Hellenic Post (ELTA)** post office is on Syndagma Square and is open 7:30am–8:30pm Mon–Fri, 7:30am–2:45pm Sat and 9am–1:30pm Sun. Around the city, smaller post offices typically work 8am–2pm Mon–Fri. Letter boxes are bright yellow.

Television and Radio

The three state-owned TV channels: ERT1 offer news and current affairs, while ERT2 and ERT3 are for entertainment and sports. All three are run by the Hellenic Broadcasting Corporation (ERT). In addition, there is a host of private channels that air soap operas, game shows, sport and films (mainly foreign productions, shown in the original version, with Greek subtitles). Most hotels have in-room TVs set on international channels such as the BBC, CNN and Euronews.

There are three main radio channels owned by the government: ERA1, offers news and current affairs; ERA2 primarily plays music; and ERA3 focuses on culture and classical music. Countless local private stations play mostly Greek music.

Newspapers and Magazines

Newsstands in the city centre stock foreign-language newspapers, though they are sometimes a day out of date. **Kathimerini**, one of the main Greek-language papers, has a sizable English-language version (online only). Another worthwhile online paper is **GreekReporter**. **LiFO** and **Athinorama**, the weekly magazines (and their respective websites) offer listings and reviews that are comprehensive, as well as articles on local topics; these are published in Greek only. Online English magazine **Greece-Is** has very high quality features and news, always worth a look.

Opening Hours

Office hours in Athens are generally 9am–5pm Mon–Fri, with some businesses closing completely during August. Banks open 8am–2:30pm during Mon–Thu and 8am–2pm Fri.

Shopping hours are a bit more complicated. Earlier, small, family-run stores worked 9am– 2:30pm Mon and Wed; 9am–2pm and 5:30–8:30pm Tue and Thu–Fri; and 9am–3pm Sat. Supermarkets follow a different routine: Mon–Fri 8am–9pm, Sat 8am–8pm. Big Athenian department stores such as Attica and Notos adhere to the same schedule. However, there are no hard and fast rules, and opening hours tend to vary from store to store. Some stores close completely in August.

Most museums are open Apr–Oct daily (times vary from museum to museum) but work for reduced hours Nov–Mar, opening Tue–Sun (closed Mon). Most archaeological sites are open daily (Apr–Oct: 8am–7/8pm daily and Nov–Mar 8am–3pm).

Most banks, stores and businesses are closed on public holidays. The list of the public holidays is as follows: New Year's Day (1 Jan), Epiphany (6 Jan), Lent Monday, Independence Day (25 Mar), Good Friday, Easter Sunday, Easter Monday, Labour Day (1 May), Whit Monday, Dormition (15 Aug), Ohi Day (28 Oct), Christmas Day (25 Dec) and 26 December.

Time Difference

Greece operates on Eastern European Time (EET), which is two hours ahead of Greenwich Mean Time (GMT) and seven hours ahead of US Eastern Standard Time (EST). The clock moves forward one hour during daylight saving time, from the last Sunday in March until the last Sunday in October.

Electrical Appliances

Greece uses thick round-pin Schuko plugs of CEE 7/3 and 7/4 standards. The Schuko power points also accept the older, narrow-pin, unearthed Europlug CEE 7/16 or 7/17, but loosely. Electrical frequency and voltage in all cases is 230 V/50Hz. UK devices will need adaptors, while North American devices will need adaptors and voltage converters. Most electrical merchants in Athens offer plug adaptors.

Driving Licences

All valid full European driving licences are accepted in Greece. If you are from outside the EU, you should get an International Driving Permit (IDP) before you leave home (from the AAA in the US or from certain post offices in the UK). To hire a car, you must be 21 years or older, and you need to have a credit card and either a passport or ID card.

Weather

A Mediterranean climate means winters are cool and summers are sunny and hot, almost rain-free. In the peak season (Jul–Aug), temperatures can soar to 40º C (104º F). The coldest months are Jan–Feb, when temperatures occasionally drop to 0º C (32º F) and snow is rare but not unknown. However, as part of climate changes observed across the world, the weather patterns in Greece have seen severe disruptions as well, so generalizations can often be quite risky.

DIRECTORY

TRAVELLERS WITH SPECIFIC NEEDS
Accessible Travel Greece
w accessibletravel.gr
Sage Traveling
w sagetraveling.com

POSTAL SERVICES
ELTA (Hellenic Post)
w elta.gr

NEWSPAPERS AND MAGAZINES
Athinorama (Greek only)
w athinorama.gr
Greece Is
w greece-is.com
Greek Reporter
w greece.greekreporter.com
Kathimerini (English version)
w ekathimerini.com
LiFO (Greek only)
w lifo.gr

Language

Greek (Ellenika) is the official language, written using the Greek alphabet. Street signs are generally posted in both Greek and Latin characters. Most young people, especially those working in tourism, speak good English.

Smoking

Smoking is prohibited in enclosed public spaces, including restaurants, nightclubs and offices (with heavy fines levied for violations), as well as in ferries and taxis. Most Greeks are, however, heavy smokers, and many bar and café owners remain hesitant to enforce non-smoking laws for fear of losing customers. If ash trays have not been placed on tables, small seashells are code that smokers are welcome and that ash trays can be asked for.

Visitor Information

The **Greek National Tourism Organization (GNTO)** has a visitor information office at Dionysiou Areopagitou 18–20, right opposite the Acropolis Museum (9am–8pm Mon–Fri, 10am–4pm Sat), which gives transport schedules and can confirm timings of museums and sites. Business travellers will appreciate the website of the **City of Athens Convention and Visitors Bureau**. Both facilities give out maps and leaflets. The official website of the **Municipality of Athens** is useful, as is the **This is Athens** website, which is run by a number of official entities.

Trips and Tours

There are countless ways to explore Athens' impressive historical sites. For private guides, contact the **Association of Licensed Tourist Guides** for a directory of qualified guides, with detailed profiles online.

You can also join the **Athens Open Tour**, which operates yellow open-top double-decker buses on a circular 90-minute tour, starting from Syndagma Square and taking in the city's main attractions, including the Acropolis, Acropolis Museum, the Benaki Museum and the National Archaeological Museum. Buses run daily, every 30 minutes (8am–7:45pm Apr–Nov and 9am–5:30pm Dec–Mar). The ticket is valid for 24 hours.

Active visitors might prefer **Athens by Bike**, which offers a guided bicycle tour around the main historic sites. **Alternative Athens** and **Alternative Tours of Athens** offer amusing and informative tours giving an insight into the local lifestyle. Canada-based **Tours by Locals** can organize local freelance guides offering specialist private tours. **Discover Greek Culture** and **Athens Insiders** are great for food, history and culture lovers.

Shopping

Shopping in Athens is fun and colourful, especially for gifts. Greek souvenirs include regional wines, olive oil, honey, *flokati* (shaggy woollen rugs), traditional copper coffee pots and handmade wooden backgammon sets. The best areas to look for these are Plaka, Thisio and Monastiraki. Replicas of Ancient Greek finds – such as ceramic vases, or gold and silver jewellery – are for sale in some museum shops. The most atmospheric shopping venue is the Central Market, a series of covered halls on Athinas, between Monastiraki Square and Omonia Square, which is a good place for local seasonal fruit and vegetables.

For designer clothing, accessories and jewellery, head for the upmarket boutiques in Kolonaki. If on a tighter budget, join the locals on pedestrian-only Ermou, which has all the big European chain-stores, such as Zara, Benetton and Promod.

Dining

Dining out is integral to socializing – Greeks generally order a selection of dishes and share them, eating, drinking and chatting for several hours, with less strictly defined courses than in most other European countries.

Go to a *psistaria* for spit-roasted and chargrilled meats, such as chops and sausages; a *souvlatzidiko* (souvlaki), *kebabtzidiko* (kebab) or *gyradiko* (gyros), served as take-away snacks, or a *mezedopolio* for small platters of *mezedes* (tasty savoury snacks) served with ouzo, *tsipouro* or carafes of *hyma* (bulk) wine. A taverna is an informal rustic eatery that serves traditional hearty cooking, while a *psarotaverna* is a taverna specializing in fish and seafood dishes. Since the crisis began, *inomageria* (old-fashioned wine-and-cookshops) have seen renewed popularity.

Greek Breakfast is an organization dedicated to reinforcing quality, regionally based breakfasts at select hotels across the country. Greeks tend to eat other meals later than most countries have theirs. Restaurants serve lunch noon–4pm and dinner 8pm–midnight. Some of the eateries serve meals all day long and do not close between lunch and dinner. To really get a look at "proper" Athenian cuisine, book a tour with **Culinary Backstreets**, with lots of sampling included en route.

Accommodation

Athens has a wide range of places to sleep. Prestigious five-star hotels with old-fashioned elegance and extras such as rooftop swimming pools are to be found around Syndagma, close to the Parliament building. For sightseeing, touristy Plaka and the adjoining areas of Koukaki and Makrygianni, are ideal bases, thanks to their proximity to the Acropolis. Here you will find midrange boutique hotels in renovated Neo-Classical buildings that have chic interiors, as well as basic but comfortable pensions and B&Bs. Likewise, Monastiraki and Psyrri have hip boutique hotels with personalized service, and crowded hostels with dormitories, in keeping with the gritty downtown scene of these neighbourhoods'. Avoid Omonia, as it is not totally safe at night, which is why there

are cheaper room prices and mediocre hotels popular with guided tour groups. Exárhia, although a bit hilly and thus challenging for those who are heavily laden, has a few worthwhile, safe hotels.

In recent years, Athens has seen the opening of a dozen or so hostels aimed at young back-packers, as well as an increasing number of locals who offer apartments to rent (along with facilities for self-catering), as well as individual rooms.

Hotels are given star ratings by the **Hellenic Chamber of Hotels**. The prices vary depending on supply and demand, with high season generally viewed as Jul–Aug, when many foreign visitors stop in Athens for a couple of nights, before heading to the Greek islands. A continental breakfast of varying quality is typically included in the rates. The Hellenic Chamber of Hotels has made efforts to promote the revival of the long-forgotten traditional Greek breakfast, which comprises yogurts, fruit, home-baked pies as well as regional specialities such as cheeses and sausages.

There are numerous websites that allow you to choose and book your choice of accommodation in Athens. **Booking.com** and **Hotelscombined. com** help you to book hotels, while **HostelWorld** is the right place to find hostels and budget accommodation. Often, though, it is a good idea to make your booking direct through the hotel. Hostel website **Airbnb** is a great resource for apartments and private rooms.

Places to Stay

PRICE CATEGORIES
For a standard, double room per night (with breakfast
if included), taxes and extra charges.
....
€ under €80   €€ €80–200   €€€ over €200

Luxury and High-End Hotels

Athenaeum Inter-Continental

MAP T2 ▪ Syngrou 89–93, Neos Kosmos ▪ 210 920 6000 ▪ www.inter continental.com ▪ €€
Well-equipped, modern and stylish, this hotel also has excellent business facilities that make it popular with executives, who also appreciate the gym, sauna, pool and shuttle to the city centre.

Radisson Blu Park Hotel

MAP D1 ▪ Leoforos Alexandras 10, Exárhia ▪ 210 889 4500 ▪ www. radissonblu.com ▪ €€
Overlooking the greenery of Pedio tou Areos, this smart hotel has 152 rooms and suites decorated in subtle hues, each with a grey marble bathroom. There is also a rooftop pool and fitness centre.

St George Lycabettus

MAP F3 ▪ Kleomenous 2, Kolonaki ▪ 210 741 6000 ▪ www.sglycabettus.gr ▪ €€
At this chic 154-room and 15-suite hotel built into the pine-scented slopes of Lykavittos Hill, full use is made of the rooftop, with an excellent restaurant, a swimming pool and a bar all sharing the great views. A minibus service will whisk you to Platia Syndagmatos.

Divani Apollon Palace & Thalasso

MAP T3 ▪ Ag. Nikolaou 10 & Iliou, Vouliagmeni ▪ 210 891 1100 ▪ www.divani-apollonhotel.com ▪ €€€
This is a vast seaside hotel that has spacious rooms adorned with oak furniture and marble bathrooms. The complex has a private beach, and there are also outdoor and indoor pools. The thalassotherapy centre located on the property is a major focus.

Divani Caravel

MAP G5 ▪ Vasileos Alexandrou 2, Pangrati ▪ 210 720 7000 ▪ www. divanicaravelhotel.com ▪ €€€
The lobby is decorated with antiques and marble, and the rooms are fitted out with every business amenity. Some 35 rooms have Acropolis views. There are bars and restaurants, and a rooftop garden with an indoor/outdoor pool, next to the gym/spa. A free shuttle takes you to Syndagma.

Electra Palace

MAP L4 ▪ Navarhou Nikodimou 18–20, Plaka ▪ 210 337 0000 ▪ www. electrahotels.gr ▪ €€€
This stylish hotel, probably the nicest in Plaka, has a mock Neo-Classical façade. The rooftop pool, with Acropolis views, is a great place to cool off after a day of sightseeing.

The Hilton

MAP F4 ▪ Vasilissis Sofias 46, Ilissia ▪ 210 728 1000 ▪ www.hilton.com ▪ €€€
The well-situated Athens Hilton is smart, functional and modern. Facilities include five restaurants, two bars (one on the rooftop), a swimming pool and a health centre, plus conference amenities.

Hotel Grande Bretagne

MAP M3 ▪ Vas. Georgiou tou Protou 1, Syndagma ▪ 210 333 0000 ▪ www. grande bretagne.gr ▪ €€€
This hotel exudes timeless luxury with its marble lobby and glittering chandeliers, along with 320 opulent rooms and suites, a rooftop restaurant and pool, and the fitness centre.

King George Palace

MAP M3 ▪ Vas. Georgiou tou Protou 3, Syndagma ▪ 210 322 2210 ▪ www. kinggeorge palace.gr ▪ €€€
A former retreat of the rich and famous, this hotel has 102 rooms and suites, all with marble bathrooms and individually furnished with select antiques.

NJV Athens Plaza

MAP M3 ▪ Vas. Georgiou tou Protou 2 & Stadiou ▪ 210 335 2400 ▪ www. njvathens plaza.gr ▪ €€€
Smack in the city centre, this hotel has designer rooms with marble bathrooms, massage showers and Bulgari toiletries, plus a famously elegant lobby. Rooms on the eighth and ninth floors have great views of the Acropolis.

Boutique and Design Hotels

Coco Mat Athens
MAP P2 ▪ Patriarhou loakeim 36, Kolonaki ▪ 210 723 0000 ▪ www. cocomat athens.com ▪ €€

The Greek mattress company Coco Mat runs several hotels showcasing its wonderful beds. This hotel has 39 rooms, all with wooden floors and fabrics in muted earthy tones, and bathrooms of grey marble or white tiles.

Emporikon Athens
MAP K3 ▪ Eolou 27A, Monastiraki ▪ 693 016 1566 ▪ www.emporikon athenshotel.com ▪ €€

The Neo-Classical Emporikon Athens Hotel is set in a refurbished 19th-century landmark building located just off vibrant Platia Agia Irinis.

InnAthens
MAP L4 ▪ Georgiou Souri 3 & Filellinon, Syndagma ▪ 210 325 8555 ▪ www. innathens.com ▪ €€

Occupying a renovated Neo-Classical mansion, InnAthens has 22 rooms and suites with marble bathrooms and slick contemporary design. It centres on a peaceful courtyard, a short walk from Syndagma. The superb breakfast is made with local Greek produce.

O&B
MAP B3 ▪ Leokoriou 7, Psyrri ▪ 210 331 2940 ▪ www.oandbhotel.com ▪ €€

This welcoming hotel prides itself on personalized service. It has just 22 rooms and suites, with minimalist design and tones of cream and beige.

The small bar-restaurant does a fantastic breakfast, as well as serves drinks and light meals all day. It is located on the boundary between Psyrri and Thisio districts, only a 20-minute walk from the Acropolis.

Pallas Athena
MAP C3 ▪ Athinas 65, Athens ▪ 210 325 0900 ▪ www.grecotelpallas athena.com ▪ €€

A luxury boutique hotel, this is situated in the centre of the city and prides itself on its great art displays. The walls of its family rooms are decorated with fun murals and the loft suites are filled with contemporary art and sculpture. The hotel has an excellent restaurant with affordable set menus, and a tasty breakfast.

Periscope Hotel
MAP P2 ▪ Haritos 22, Kolonaki ▪ 210 729 7200 ▪ www.periscope.athens hotels.it ▪ €€

A minimalist-style hotel, Periscope is located on a quiet street. The rooms get better on the higher floors in the building. The rooftop periscope (hence the name) scans the city and projects images in the lobby bistro.

Semiramis Hotel
MAP T2 ▪ Harilaou Trikoupi 48, Kefalari, Kifissia ▪ 210 628 4400 ▪ www.yeshotels.gr/ semiramis ▪ €€

Dominant colours in this funky 51-room hotel, designed by Karim Rashid are orange, pink and lime-green. There's a heated outdoor pool and a fitness centre. A changing selection of contemporary art is displayed in the lobby.

AthensWas
MAP K5 ▪ Dionysiou Areopagitou 5, Makrygianni ▪ 210 924 9954 ▪ www. athenswas.gr ▪ €€€

This 21-room hotel stands on a traffic-free promenade, a short walk from the Acropolis Museum. It's furnished with pieces by important 20th-century designers such as Le Corbusier and Eileen Gray, giving it a retro-chic vibe. The bathrooms are slick and spacious; the cooked-to-order breakfast is delicious. The rooftop restaurant at the hotel has the Acropolis immediately opposite it.

The Margi Hotel
MAP T3 ▪ Litous 11, Vouliagmeni ▪ 210 892 9000 ▪ www.the-margi.gr ▪ €€€

A five-minute walk from Vouliagmeni beach, this gem of a hotel has 89 rooms and suites, decorated in warm hues, with 19th-century antiques and marble bathrooms. Guests relax on poolside daybeds, and there is an excellent nouvelle cuisine restaurant on site.

New Hotel
MAP L4 ▪ Filellinon 16, Syndagma ▪ 210 327 3000 ▪ www.yeshotels. gr/newhotel ▪ €€€

New Hotel stands a short walk from Syndagma. Its 79 rooms feature bamboo floors and quirky recycled furniture created by the Campana brothers from Brazil. Cooked-to-order breakfast as well as the Sunday brunch are served in the New Taste restaurant, while later meals are served at the rooftop bar-bistro.

Mid-Range Hotels

Nefeli
MAP L4 ▪ Yperidou 16, Plaka ▪ 210 322 8044 ▪ www.hotel-nefeli. com ▪ €
Located on a quiet pedestrian zone, Nefeli has 18 well maintained rooms; many have balconies. Breakfasts at the hotel are very good and the staff is friendly.

Acropolis Select
MAP C6 ▪ Falirou 37–9, Koukaki ▪ 210 921 1610 ▪ www.acropoliselect.gr ▪ €€
One of the best deals in town: for only a little more than a budget hotel, you get a stylish lobby, a skylit restaurant, comfortable rooms, satellite TV, business amenities and Acropolis views. It is a short walk from most of the tourist sights.

A for Athens
MAP J3 ▪ Miaouli 2–4, Monastiraki ▪ 210 324 4244 ▪ www.aforathens. com ▪ €€
This boutique hotel with a contemporary design ethos and 35 rooms (including family quads) is just across from the Acropolis, so guests enjoy unique views of this ancient monument even while they take a shower.

Athens Center Square
MAP J2 ▪ Aristogeitonos 15, Monastiraki ▪ 210 322 2706 ▪ www.athens centresquarehotel.gr ▪ €€
Located downtown opposite the Central Market, this friendly, welcoming hotel has 54 colour-themed rooms with wooden floors, and a rooftop terrace with good views of the Acropolis and Lykavittos Hill. The price includes a generous buffet breakfast.

Central Hotel
MAP L3 ▪ Apollonos 21, Syndagma ▪ 210 323 4357 ▪ www.central hotel.gr ▪ €€
Modern, minimalist and smart, the Central is one of the most reasonably priced hotels for its quality and location. Relax in the rooftop whirlpool with a view of the Acropolis and the mountains beyond.

Hermes
MAP L3 ▪ Apollonos 19, Syndagma ▪ 210 322 2706 ▪ www.hermes hotel.gr ▪ €€
The Hermes has 45 rooms with wooden floors and cheerful, contemporary design. Some of the rooms are interconnected, which makes them ideal for families. There is also a playroom for small kids. A large buffet breakfast, based on typical Greek produce, or a pre-dawn service for early departers, is included.

Herodion
MAP C6 ▪ Rovertou Galli 4, Makrygianni ▪ 210 923 6832 ▪ www.herodion.gr ▪ €€
In a quiet neighbourhood just below the Acropolis, this attractive, modern hotel has comfortable if small rooms. It does manage to score the highest for its common areas: a ground-floor breakfast area with a landscaped conservatory, and a roof garden with two whirlpools, eyefuls of the Acropolis plus yoga and massage on request.

Hotel Plaka
MAP K3 ▪ Kapnikareas 7 & Mitropoleos, Monastiraki ▪ 210 322 2706 ▪ www.plakahotel. gr ▪ €€
This hotel represents excellent value – for its unbeatable location between Plaka and the shopping street of Ermou, as well as for its warm and simple but stylish rooms in three grades. The roof garden offers a view of the Acropolis.

Philippos Hotel
MAP K6 ▪ Mitseon 3, Makrygianni ▪ 210 922 3611 ▪ www.philippos hotel.gr ▪ €€
In a peaceful residential side street, close to the Acropolis Museum, the Herodion's sister hotel is welcoming, peaceful and comfortable. The 50 rooms and suites are light and airy – most have balconies, some have Acropolis views. The continental breakfast is adequate, and there are rooftop and atrium bistros.

Ava
MAP L5 ▪ Lysikratous 9–11, Plaka ▪ 210 325 9000 ▪ www.avahotel.gr ▪ €€€
Known for its high service standards, this hotel has smaller units for couples and big suites for families of four. Some of the higher units have oblique views of the Acropolis.

Budget Hotels and Hostels

Art Gallery Hotel
MAP C6 ▪ Erechthiou 5, Koukaki ▪ 210 923 8376 ▪ www.artgalleryhotel.gr ▪ €
Priciest in the budget options, this hotel is a

short walk from the Acropolis. It has wooden parquet floors and art in every room, though three bathrooms are down the hall. Off-season monthly rates are low, and breakfast is extra.

Athens Backpackers
MAP L5 ▪ Makri 12, Makrygianni ▪ 210 922 4044 ▪ www.backpackers. gr ▪ €
At this hostel, there are dorms with three to six beds, and the ensuing social life makes it hugely popular. They also have an annexe, Athens Studios.

Athens Choice
MAP C2 ▪ Veranzerou 45, Omonia ▪ 210 523 8738 ▪ www.athens choice.com ▪ €
This hostel has a modern minimalist look in greys and charcoal. Available room types include private rooms and shared dorms (sleeping four). There is a bar, TV lounge and laundry service, plus breakfast is included. It's a five-minute walk from the Omonia metro station; in addition, Exarhia and the National Archaeological Museum are not too far away.

City Circus Hostel
MAP J2 ▪ Sarri 16, Psyrri ▪ 213 023 7244 ▪ www. citycircus.gr ▪ €
In a renovated Neo-Classical mansion with frescoed ceilings, wrought-iron balconies and vintage furniture, retro-chic City Circus is a five-minute walk from Monastiraki metro station. It has private doubles and shared dorms sleeping four, six or eight, a restaurant and a roof terrace with a view of the Acropolis.

Hotel Exarchion
MAP D2 ▪ Themistokleous 55, Exárhia ▪ 210 380 0731 ▪ www. exarchion.com ▪ €
A good budget option, Hotel Exarchion has balconies in most of its rooms. Breakfasts at the first-floor lounge are quite good. There is also a sidewalk café that is good for people watching, along with a roof bar with views of Lykavittos hill.

Hotel Phaedra
MAP L5 ▪ Cherefontos 16, Plaka ▪ 210 323 8461 ▪ www.hotelphaedra. com ▪ €
Known for its friendly staff, this 21-room family-run hotel features balconies overlooking a Byzantine church or the Acropolis. The rooms are tastefully appointed, and some have private bathrooms that are located across the hall. The rooftop terrace of the Phaedra is a great place for its magnificent views.

Marble House Pension
MAP B6 ▪ Alley off Anastasiou Zinni 35, Koukaki ▪ 210 922 8294 ▪ www.marble house.gr ▪ €
A favourite of students as well as artists, and very peacefully set on a dead-end lane, Marble House has clean, simple rooms and a friendly atmosphere. It offers discounted tours and monthly rates in the off season. Be aware that some of the rooms here share a bathroom down the hall. Breakfast is extra, and service from the managing family is kind. It is mandatory to make reservations in advance of your stay.

Orion-Dryades
MAP D2 ▪ Emmanouil Benaki 105 and Anexartisias ▪ 210 330 2387 ▪ www.orion-dryades.com ▪ €
These Siamese-Twin co-managed hotels, sitting peacefully above the buzz of Exárhia on Stgrefi Hill, are a long-standing, safe favourite for those seeking budget accommodation. Breakfast is served at the Orion, where the reception is located. There is a stiff climb uphill, so take a taxi if heavily laden.

Tempi Hotel
MAP J2 ▪ Aiolou 29, Monastiraki ▪ 210 321 3175 ▪ www.tempi hotel.gr ▪ €
This family-run budget hotel is located near Platía Agias Irinis, and is also close to major attractions. The rooms are simple and comfortable, and 14 of the 24 rooms have en suite bathrooms. A roof terrace, a communal kitchen and the facility of free luggage storage are major pluses.

Athens Studios
MAP K6 ▪ Veïkou 3A, Makrygianni ▪ 210 923 5811 ▪ www.athens studios.gr ▪ €€
Co-managed with Athens Backpackers, this is even closer to the Acropolis Museum. Room types include private studios and apartments (sleeping from two to six) that are ideal for couples or families and come with fully equipped kitchens and small en suite bathrooms. Shared dorms that accommodate up to six people are also an option. The tariff includes a continental breakfast.

For a key to hotel price categories see p144

High-End Hotels Outside Athens

Kastalia Boutique Hotel
MAP Q1 ■ Vasileos Pavlou ke Friderikis 13, Delphi ■ 226 508 2205 ■ www.kastaliahotel.gr ■ €
Set in a Neo-Classical mansion, this boutique hotel is close to Delphi's archaeological site. It has 28 rooms and suites, as well as a lounge with an open fireplace. Breakfast is served on the stone terrace, with views of the Plistos gorge and the sea.

Bratsera
MAP S4 ■ Harbour, Hydra ■ 229 805 3971 ■ Mar–Oct ■ www.bratserahotel.com ■ €€
This hotel housed in a former sponge factory is one of the most charming places to stay on Hydra. The best units are junior suites, some with private terraces. There are also quads for families. The very deep pool (where sponges were rinsed at one time) is the only one of its kind in town.

Orloff Boutique Hotel
MAP S4 ■ Rafalia 9, Platia Nikolaou Votsi, Hydra port ■ 229 805 2564 ■ www.orloff.gr ■ €€
All the rooms at Hydra's first boutique hotel are unique in layout; some overlook the town, others the breakfast courtyard. The premium suite fits parents and two kids.

Amphitryon Hotel
MAP R3 ■ Spiliadou, Nafplio ■ 275 207 0700 ■ www.amphitryon.gr ■ €€€
Situated in Nafplio's Old Town, this smart hotel overlooks the sea, with a view of the Bourtzi (fortified islet). The 45 contemporary rooms and suites have wooden floors and marble-tiled bathrooms, while the Circle restaurant serves Mediterranean cuisine.

Elatos Resort & Health Club
MAP R1 ■ Itamos, nr Arachova ■ 223 406 1162 ■ www.elatos resort.gr ■ €€€
Greece's only alpine resort is set in a pine forest at the edge of Parnassos National Park. All 40 chalets have two to three bedrooms, kitchens, fireplaces and verandas. The central buildings offer a fully equipped health club, bar and restaurant.

Grand Resort Lagonissi
MAP T3 ■ 40th km on the Athens–Sounio road, Lagonissi ■ 229 107 6000 ■ www.lagonissiresort.gr ■ €€€
This vast resort complex spreads out over its own peninsula between Sounio and Vouliagmeni. The resort encompasses 16 beaches, a range of seafront suites and lavish villas that have their own pools. There are also a host of restaurants and organized activities.

Grecotel Cape Sounio
MAP T3 ■ 67th km on the Athens–Sounio Rd ■ 229 206 9700 ■ www.capesounio.com ■ €€€
Offering all the mod cons you would expect in its bungalows and villas, this hotel is set on a verdant hillside, with spectacular views of the sea and the Temple of Poseidon.

Orloff Resort
Off map ■ Spetses ■ 229 807 5444 ■ www.orloffresort.com ■ €€€
This stylish boutique hotel is housed in a 19th-century mansion with an outdoor pool. The 19 rooms, studios and apartments combine traditional Greek architecture with modern and minimalist design.

Thermae Sylla Grand Hotel
MAP S1 ■ Edipsos, North Evvia ■ 222 606 0100 ■ www.thermaesylla.gr ■ €€€
One of the best spas in Greece, the Thermae Sylla offers treatments featuring local restorative mineral-laden spring waters, as well as with a wide array of beauty and relaxation treatments. The Belle Epoque external architecture has been preserved; but the rooms and treatment areas are fully modern.

Wyndham Poseidon Resort
MAP R2 ■ Loutraki Korinthias, Loutraki ■ 274 406 7938 ■ www.wyndhamloutrakiresort.com ■ €€€
This resort has a small private beach and extensive gardens, as well as sporting, spa and conference facilities. Options for accommodation comprise 13 grades of suites, which range from a junior suite with a garden view to a presidential seafront suite; most of the suites can accommodate four people. All suites share wooden flooring but not much else, so be sure that you read the room descriptions carefully.

Mid and Budget Outside Athens

Aeginitiko Archontiko
MAP S3 ▪ Thomaidou 1 & Agiou Nikolaou, Egina Town ▪ 2297 024 968 ▪ www.aeginitiko-archontiko.gr ▪ €
A 19th-century mansion, this has painted ceilings upstairs, a parlour with stained-glass windows, and a garden courtyard. A dozen rooms are small and clean.

Alkyoni
MAP S3 ▪ Skala, south end on clifftop, Angistri ▪ 229 709 1377 ▪ www.alkyoni-agistri.com ▪ €
With a tranquil location, this hotel has flagstoned, ground-floor doubles and better specced rooms upstairs for families. The terrace restaurant is one of the better places to eat on Angistri.

Byron
MAP R3 ▪ Platonos 2, Platia Agiou Spyridona ▪ 275 202 2351 ▪ www.byronhotel.gr ▪ €
The first of Nafplion's boutique hotels, this is still one of the best. Many rooms overlook a domed Ottoman hammam; some have balconies. The units are scattered over two buildings. The breakfasts are very good.

Hotel Belle Helene
MAP R3 ▪ Through road, centre of modern village, Mycenae ▪ 275 107 6225 ▪ €
German archaeologist Heinrich Schliemann stayed here (in room No. 3) in the 1870s, and many a famous figure (including top Nazis) has followed in his footsteps.

Modern-day tourists can enjoy comfortable, clean and quiet rooms, though the bathrooms are located down the hall because of concerns for preservation.

Likoria
MAP R1 ▪ West edge of town, Venizelou ▪ 226 703 2132 ▪ www.likoria.gr ▪ €
This comfortable hotel is open in summer and winter. With sauna and hammam, it is aimed at skiers. The best rooms have a view and a fireplace. It's a good choice for drivers as street parking is possible here, unlike in central Arahova.

Orfeas
MAP Q1 ▪ Ifigenias Syngrou 35, Delphi ▪ 226 508 2777 ▪ www.hotelorfeas.com ▪ €
A small, friendly, family-run hotel, this is on a quiet upper street away from the noisy main thoroughfares but still walkable to almost everything. Breakfast here is better than the star category (2) would suggest. Top-floor rooms are best for appointment and views.

Archontiko Art Hotel
MAP Q1 ▪ Hillside beyond Hirolakkas cove, Galaxidi ▪ 2265 042 292 ▪ www.hotels-in-galaxidi.gr ▪ €€
The eight themed rooms here sound a little kitschy but most manage to work. The "Bridal" has a huge canopy bed draped with sheer white linen; the "At Sea" is decorated like a boat; while adventurous couples often choose the "Conception", featuring a round bed and mirrored ceiling. When not enjoying their rooms, guests can stroll in the garden.

Hotel Ganimede
MAP Q1 ▪ Nikolaou Gourgouri 20, Galaxidi ▪ 226 504 1328 ▪ www.ganimede.gr ▪ €€
This 19th-century mansion has six simple but elegant doubles, a modern family suite across the courtyard garden, and another one that is more remote, along with studios. The Papalexis family are excellent hosts, and the breakfasts feature homemade jams and bread straight from their family bakery. Reservations are mandatory all year, more so on weekends.

Klymeni Traditional Homes
MAP R3 ▪ 25th Martiou & Karamanli, Nafplio ▪ 275 209 6194 ▪ www.klymeni.gr ▪ €€
Offering accommodation in a range of rustic-chic studios, bungalows and apartments built of local natural stone, Klymeni is set in gardens with a barbecue, a hot tub and a children's play area. Surrounded by peaceful rural farmland, it's 1.5 km (1 mile) southeast of town, off the castle road.

Pension Marianna
MAP R3 ▪ Ilia Potamianou 9, Nafplio ▪ 2752 024 256 ▪ www.hotelmarianna.gr ▪ €€
Located in the car-free Old Town of Nafplio, this welcoming inn is quaint and romantic. Centered around a lovely courtyard, its 20 rooms are in warm shades of yellow, orange and red. A homemade 'organic' breakfast (extra charge) is served on a rooftop patio that is right below the fortress, with lovely views over the town to the Argolid Gulf.

For a key to hotel price categories see p144

General Index

Acknowledgments

Author
Coral Davenport and Jane Foster are freelance travel and features writers, based in Athens.

Additional contributors
Marc Dubin, Cordelia Madden

Publishing Director Georgina Dee

Publisher Vivien Antwi

Design Director Phil Ormerod

Editorial Michelle Crane, Rachel Fox, Freddie Marriage, Adrian Potts, Sally Schafer, Sands Publishing Solutions, Hollie Teague

Cover Design Maxine Pedliham, Vinita Venugopal

Design Marisa Renzullo, Stuti Tiwari, Vinita Venugopal

Picture Research Ellen Root, Lucy Sienkowska, Rituraj Singh

Cartography Mohammad Hassan, Zafar-ul-Islam Khan, Suresh Kumar, James Macdonald, John Plumer

DTP Jason Little, Azeem Siddiqui

Production Luca Bazzoli

Factchecker Marisa Tejada

Proofreader Clare Peel

Indexer Hilary Bird

First edition created by Blue Island Publishing, London

Revisions Shikha Kulkarni, Gaurav Nagpal, Bandana Paul, Anuroop Sanwalia, Azeem Siddiqui

Commissioned Photography Courtesy of ARF/TAP (Archaeological Receipts Fund), Nigel Hicks, Courtesy of Kori 69b, Rob Reichenfeld, Rough Guides/Chris Christoforo, Rough Guides/Michelle Grant.

68tr,130b; Yoemll 34tl; Angel Yordanov 123b.
Epikouros Restaurant - Taverna: 119cr.
Folli Follie: www.imagepro.gr/S
Efstathopoulos 105t
Getty Images: AFP PHOTO/Louisa Gouliamaki
21bc; Allan Baxter 4cl, 58-9; DEA /A. Garozzo
79clb, /G. Nimatallah 18cl, /G. Dagli Orti 21crb;
Lonely Planet Images 78cla; Slow Images
86cla; George Tsafos 88crb; Universal Images
Group 11cr.
**Nicholas P Goulandris Foundation - Museum
of Cycladic Art:** 10bl, 22cla, 22c, 22br, 22-3,
23ca, 56tl.
HELLENIC FESTIVAL S.A.: 72br.
Hilton Athens: Galaxy Bar & Restaurant 106t,
Milos Restaurant 107cr.
Hytra: Kaplanidis Yirgos 67cl.
iStockphoto.com: efesenko 125cla.
Loumidis Coffee Shop: 97tl.
Marinos Restaurant: Lena Lo 127cl.
Martinos Antiques: 89tr.
**Melissinos Art - The Poet
Sandalmaker:** 89bc.
Rakadiko Stoa Kouvelou: 112br.
Restaurant Spondi: 67tl.
Rex by Shutterstock: De Agostini/G. Dagli Orti
92tl; Sharok Hatami 41br.
Rififi: 67br, 98br.
Robert Harding Picture Library: Massimo
Pizzotti 20bl; Silwen Randebrock 26tr.
Photo Scala, Florence: 32cr; DeAgostini
Picture Library/Veneranda Biblioteca
Ambrosiana 55cl.
Six D.O.G.S: 91tl.
Skoumoky: 81t.
SuperStock: LatitudeStock/Capture Ltd 73tr.
The New Acropolis Museum: Giorgos
Vitsaropoulos 82b.
Warehouse: Themis Katsimihas 98cl.
War Museum, Athens: 49br.
WeArePress: 66cla.

Cover

Front and spine: **AWL Images:** Doug Pearson.
Back: **AWL Images:** Doug Pearson bc, Ken
Scicluna cla; **Dreamstime.com:** Petr Goskov tl,
Bo Li tr, Napa735 crb.

Pull Out Map Cover

AWL Images: Doug Pearson
All other images © Dorling Kindersley
For further information see:
www.dkimages.com

*As a guide to abbreviations in visitor information
blocks:* **Adm** = *admission charge;* **D** = *dinner;*
L = *lunch.*

Penguin
Random
House

Printed and bound in China

First edition in 2004

Published in Great Britain by
Dorling Kindersley Limited
80 Strand, London WC2R 0RL

Published in the United States by
DK Publishing, 1450 Broadway, Suite 801,
New York, NY 10018, USA

Copyright © 2004, 2019 Dorling
Kindersley Limited

A Penguin Random House Company

19 20 21 22 10 9 8 7 6 5 4 3 2 1

**Reprinted with revisions 2006, 2008, 2010,
2012, 2014, 2017, 2019**

ISSN 1479-344X

ISBN 978-0-2413-6473-4

MIX
Paper from
responsible sources
FSC™ C018179

Phrase Book

In an Emergency

Help!	Voithia!	vo-ee-theea
Stop!	Stamatíste!	sta-ma-tee-steh
Call a doctor!	Fonáxte éna giatró!	fo-nak-steh e-na ya-tro
Call an ambulance/ the police/	Kaléste to asthenofóro/tin astynomía/tin	ka-le-steh to as-the-no-fo-ro teen a-sti-no-the mia/ teen pee-ro-zve-stee-kee!
fire brigade!	pyrosvestikí!	poo ee-ne to
Where is the nearest telephone/ hospital/ pharmacy?	Poú eínai to plisiéstero tiléfono / nosokomeío / farmakeío?	plee-see-e-ste-ro tee-le-pho-no/ no-so-ko-mee-o/ far-ma-kee-o

Communication Essentials

Yes	Nai	neh
No	Ohi	o-hee
Please	Parakaló	pa-ra-ka-lo
Thank you	Efharistó	ef-ha-ree-sto
You are welcome	Parakaló	pa-ra-ka-lo
OK/alright	Endáxei	en-dak-zee
Excuse me	Me synchoreíte	me seen-cho-ree-teh
Hello	Giá sas	yeea sas
Goodbye	Andío	an-dee-o
Good morning	Kaliméra	ka-lee-me-ra
Good night	Kalinýhta	ka-lee-neech-ta
Morning	Proí	pro-ee
Afternoon	Apógevma	a-po-yev-ma
Evening	Vrádi	vrath-i
This morning	Símera to proí	see-me-ra to pro-ee
Yesterday	Chthés	chthes
Today	Símera	see-me-ra
Tomorrow	Avrio	av-ree-o
Here	Edó	ed-o
There	Ekeí	e-kee
What?	Tí?	tee
Why?	Giatí?	ya-tee
Where?	Poú?	poo
How?	Pós?	pos
Wait!	Perímene!	pe-ree-me-neh
How are you?	Tí káneis?	tee ka-nees
Very well, thank you.	Polý kalá, efharistó.	po-lee ka-la, ef-cha-ree-sto
How do you do?	Pós eíste?	pos ees-te
Pleased to meet you.	Hero polý.	che-ro po-lee
What is your name?	Pós légeste?	pos le-ye-ste
	Where is/are…?	Poú eínai…? poo ee-ne
How far is it to…?	Póso apéhei…?	po-so a-pe-chee
How do I get to…?	Pós boró na páo…?	pos bo-ro na pa-o
Do you speak English?	Miláte Angliká?	mee-la-te an-glee-ka
I understand.	Katalavaíno.	ka-ta-la-ve-no
I don't understand.	Den katalavaíno.	then ka-ta-la-ve-no
Could you speak slowly?	Miláte lígo pio argá parakaló?	mee-la-te lee-go pyo ar-ga pa-ra-ka-lo
I'm sorry.	Me synchoreíte.	me seen-cho-ree-teh

Does anyone have a key?	Ehei kanis kleidí?	e-chee ka-ne-es klee-dee

Useful Words

big	Megálo	me-ga-lo
small	Mikró	mi-kro
hot	Zestó	zes-to
cold	Krýo	kree-o
good	Kaló	ka-lo
bad	Kakó	ka-ko
enough	Arketá	ar-ke-ta
well	Kalá	ka-la
open	Anoihtá	a-neech-ta
closed	Kleistá	klee-sta
left	Aristerá	a-ree-ste-ra
right	Dexiá	dek-see-a
straight on	Efthía	ef-thee-a
between	Anámesa / Metaxý	a-na-me-sa/ me-tak-see
on the corner of…	Sti gonía tou…	stee go-nee-a too
near	Kondá	kon-da
far	Makriá	ma-kree-a
up	Epáno	e-pa-no
down	Káto	ka-to
early	Norís	no-rees
late	Argá	ar-ga
entrance	I ísodos	ee ee-so-thos
exit	I éxodos	ee ek-so-dos
toilet occupied/ engaged	I toualétes / Kateiliméni	ee too-a-le-tes ka-tee-lee-me-nee
unoccupied	Eléftheri	e-lef-the-ree
free/no charge	Doreán	tho-re-an
in/out	Mésa/ Exo	me-sa/ek-so

Making a Telephone Call

Where is the nearest public telephone?	Poú vrísketai o plisiésteros tilefonikós thálamos?	poo vrees-ke-teh o plee-see-e-ste-ros tee-le-fo-ni-kos tha-la-mos
I would like to place a long-distance call.	Tha íthela na káno éna yperastikó tilefónima.	tha ee-the-la na ka-no e-na ee-pe-ra-sti-ko tee-le-fo-nee-ma.
I would like to reverse the charges.	Tha íthela na chreóso to tilefónima ston paralípti.	tha ee-the-la na chre-o-so to tee-le-fo-nee-ma ston pa-ra-lep-tee
I will try again later.	Tha xanatilefoníso argótera.	tha ksa-na-tee-le-fo-ni-so ar-go-te-ra
Can I leave a message?	Mporeíte na tou afísete éna mínyma?	bo-ree-te na too a-fee-se-teh e-na mee-nee-ma
Could you speak up a little please?	Miláte dynatótera, parakaló?	mee-la-teh dee-na-to-te-ra, pa-ra-ka-lo
Hold on.	Periménete.	pe-ri-me-ne-teh
local call	Topikó tilefónima	to-pi-ko tee-le-fo-nee-ma
phone box/ kiosk	O tilefonikós thálamos	o tee-le-fo-ni-kos tha-la-mos
phone card	I tilekárta	ee tee-le-kar-ta

Shopping

How much does this cost?	Póso kánei?	po-so ka-nee

I would like...	Tha íthela...	tha ee-the-la
Do you have...?	Ehete...?	e-che-teh
I am just looking.	Aplós koitáo.	a-plos kee-ta-o
Do you take credit cards	Décheste pistotikés kártes	the-ches-teh pee-sto-tee-kes kar-tes
What time do you open/ close?	Póte anoígete/ klínete?	po-teh a-nee-ye-teh/ klee-ne-teh
Can you ship this overseas?	Boreíte na to steílete sto exoterikó?	bo-ree-teh na to stee-le-teh sto e-xo-te-ree-ko
This one.	Aftó edó.	af-to e-do
That one.	Ekeíno.	e-kee-no
expensive	Akrivó	a-kree-vo
cheap	Fthinó	fthee-no
size	To mégethos	to me-ge-thos
white	Lefkó	lef-ko
black	Mávro	mav-ro
red	Kókkino	ko-kee-no
yellow	Kítrino	kee-tree-no
green	Prásino	pra-see-no
blue	Mple	bleh

Sightseeing

tourist information	O EOT	o E-OT
tourist police	I touristikí astynomía	ee too-rees-tee-kee a-stee-no-mee-a
closed on public holidays	kleistó tis argíes	klee-sto tees aryee-es

Transport

When does the ... leave?	Póte févgei to...?	po-teh fev-yee to
Where is the bus stop?	Poú eínai i stási tou leoforeíou?	poo ee-neh ee sta-see too le-o-fo-ree-oo
Is there a bus to...?	Ypárhei leoforeío gia...?	ee-par-chee le-o-fo-ree-o yia
ticket office	Ekdotíria isitiríon	Ek-tho-tee-reea ee-see-tee-ree-on
return ticket	Isitírio me epistrofí	ee-see-tee-ree-o meh e-pee-stro-fee
single journey	Apló isitírio	a-plo ee-see-tee-reeo
bus station	O stathmós tou KTEL	o stath-mos too KTEL
bus ticket	Isitírio leoforíou	ee-see-tee-ree-o leo-fo-ree-oo
trolley bus	To trólley	to tro-le-ee
port	To limáni	to lee-ma-nee
train/metro	To tréno	to tre-no
railway station	sidirodromikós stathmós	see-tho-ro-thro-mee-kos stath-mos
scooter/ motorbike	papaki/ To mihanáki	pa-pa-kee/ to-mee-cha-na-kee
bicycle	To podílato	to po-thee-la-to
taxi	To taxí	to tak-see
airport	To aerodrómio	to a-e-ro-thro-mee-o
ferry	To "ferry-boat"	to fe-ree-bot
hydrofoil	To delfíni/ To ydroptérygo	to del-fee-nee/ To ee-throp-te-ree-go

catamaran for hire	To katamarán Enoikiázontai	to catamaran e-nee-kya-zon-deh

Staying in a Hotel

Do you have a vacant room?	Ehete domátia?	e-he-teh tho-ma-tee-a
I have a reservation.	Echo kánei krátisi.	e-cho ka-nee kra-tee-see.
double room with double bed	Díklino me dipló kreváti	thee-klee-no meh thee-plo kre-va-tee
twin room	Díklino me moná krevátia	thee-klee-no meh mo-na kre-vat-ya
single room	Monóklino	mo-no-klee-no
room with a bath	Domátio me mpánio	tho-ma-tee-o meh ban-yo
shower	To douz	To dooz
bathtub	Baniéra	Ban-yeh-ra
porter	O portiéris	o por-tye-rees
key	To kleidí	to klee-dee
room with a sea view/balcony	Domátio me théa sti thálassa/ balkóni	tho-ma-tee-o meh the-a stee tha-la-sa/bal-ko-nee
Does the price include breakfast?	To proïnó symperi- lamvánetai stin timí?	to pro-ee-no seem-be-ree-lam-va-ne-teh steen tee-me

Eating Out

Have you got a table?	Ehete trapézi?	e-che-te tra-pe-zee
I want to reserve a table.	Thélo na kratíso éna trapézi.	the-lo na kra-tee-so e-na tra-pe-zee
The bill, please.	Ton logariazmó parakaló.	ton lo-gar-yaz-mo pa-ra-ka-lo
I am a vegetarian.	Ímai hortofágos.	ee-meh chor-to-fa-gos
waiter/waitress	Servitóros/ servitóra	ser-vee-tor-oz/ ser-vee-tor-ah
menu	O katálogos	o ka-ta-lo-gos
cover charge	To "couvert"	to koo-ver
wine list	Lísta krasión	lees-ta kra-si-on
glass	To potíri	to po-tee-ree
bottle	To poukáli	to bou-ka-lee
knife	To mahéri	to ma-he-ree
fork	To pirouni	to pee-roo-nee
spoon	To koutáli	to koo-ta-lee
breakfast	To proïnó	to pro-ee-no
lunch	To mesi- merianó	to me-see-mer-ya-no
dinner	To dípno	to theep-no
main course	To kyríos piáto	to kee-ree-os pya-toe
starters/ first courses	Ta orektiká	ta o-rek-tee-ka
dessert	To epidórpia	eh-pee-dor-pee-ah
dish of the day	To piáto tis iméras	to pya-to tees ee-me-ras
bar	To "bar"	To bar
taverna	I tavérna	ee ta-ver-na
café	To kafenío	to ka-fe-nee-o
fish taverna	I psarotavérna	ee psa-ro-ta-ver-na
grill house	I psistariá	ee psee-sta-rya

wine-and-cookhouse	**To inomagerío**	to ee-no-ma-ye-rio		30	**triánda**	tree-an-da
dairy shop	**To galakto-poleío**	to ga-lak-to-po-lee-o		40	**saránda**	sa-ran-da
restaurant	**To estiatório**	to e-stee-a-to-ree-o		50	**penínda**	pe-neen-da
				60	**exínda**	ek-seen-da
ouzeri	**To ouzerí**	to oo-ze-ree		70	**evdomínda**	ev-tho-meen-da
meze house	**To meze-dopolío**	To me-ze-do-po-lee-o		80	**ogdónda**	og-thon-da
take away souvláki stall	**Ena souvlatzí-diko**	Eh-na soo-vlat-zee-dee-ko		90	**enenínda**	e-ne-neen-da
				100	**ekató**	e-ka-to
take away kebab stall	**Ena kebabtzí-diko**	Eh-na keh-bahb-zee-dee-ko		200	**diakósia**	thya-kos-ya
take away gyros stall	**Ena gyrádiko**	Eh-na yeer-ah-dee-ko		1,000	**hília**	cheel-ya
				2,000	**dýo hiliádes**	thee-o cheel-ya-thes
rare	**Eláhista psiméno**	e-lach-ees-ta psee-me-no		1,000,000	**éna ekatommýrio**	e-na e-ka-to-mee-ree-o
medium	**Métria psiméno**	met-ree-a psee-me-no		one minute	**éna leptó**	e-na lep-to
well done	**Kalopsiméno**	ka-lo-psee-me-no		one hour	**mía óra**	mee-a o-ra
				half an hour	**misí óra**	mee-see o-ra
Basic Food and Drink				quarter of an hour	**éna tétarto**	e-na te-tar-to
coffee	**O Kafés**	o ka-fes		half past one	**mía kai misí**	mee-a keh mee-see
with milk	**me gála**	me ga-la				
coffee without sugar	**skétos horís záhar**	ske-tos ho-rees za-ha-ree		quarter past one	**mía kai tétarto**	mee-a keh te-tar-to
medium sweet	**métrios**	me-tree-os		ten past one	**mía kai déka**	mee-a keh the-ka
very sweet	**glykós**	glee-kos				
tea	**tsái**	tsa-ee		quarter to two	**dýo pará tétarto**	thee-o pa-ra te-tar-to
hot chocolate	**zestí sokoláta**	ze-stee so-ko-la-ta		ten to two	**dýo pará déka**	thee-o pa-ra the-ka
wine	**krasí**	kra-see				
red	**kókkino**	ko-kee-no		a day	**mía méra**	mee-a me-ra
white	**lefkó**	lef-ko		a week	**mía evdomáda**	mee-a ev-tho-ma-tha
rosé	**rozé**	ro-ze				
water	**To neró**	to ne-ro		a month	**énas mínas**	e-nas mee-nas
octopus	**To chtapódi**	to chta-po-dee		a year	**énas hrónos**	e-nas hro-nos
fish	**To psári**	to psa-ree		Monday	**Deftéra**	thef-te-ra
cheese	**To tyrí**	to tee-ree		Tuesday	**Tríti**	tree-tee
halloumi	**To haloúmi**	to ha-loo-mee		Wednesday	**Tetárti**	te-tar-tee
bread	**To psomí**	to pso-mee		Thursday	**Pémpti**	pemp-tee
fava purée	**I fáva**	ee fah-va		Friday	**Paraskeví**	pa-ras-ke-vee
halva	**O halvás**	o hal-vas		Saturday	**Sávvato**	sa-va-to
meat slabs	**O gýros**	o yee-ros		Sunday	**Kyriakí**	keer-ee-a-kee
mince risolles	**Kebab**	ke-bahb		January	**Ianouários**	ee-a-noo-a-ree-os
Turkish delight	**To loukoúmi**	to loo-koo-mee				
baklava	**O baklavás**	o bak-la-vas		February	**Fevrouários**	fev-roo-a-ree-os
				March	**Mártios**	mar-tee-os
Numbers				April	**Aprílios**	a-pree-lee-os
1	**éna**	e-na		May	**Máïos**	ma-ee-os
2	**dýo**	thee-o		June	**Ioúnios**	ee-oo-nee-os
3	**tría**	tree-a		July	**Ioúlios**	ee-oo-lee-os
4	**téssera**	te-se-ra		August	**Ávgoustos**	av-goo-stos
5	**pénde**	pen-deh		September	**Septémvrios**	sep-tem-vree-os
6	**éxi**	ek-si		October	**Októvrios**	ok-to-vree-os
7	**eptá**	ep-ta		November	**Noémvrios**	no-em-vree-os
8	**ohtó**	och-to		December	**Dekémvrios**	the-kem-vree-os
9	**ennéa**	e-ne-a				
10	**déka**	the-ka				
11	**énteka**	en-de-ka				
12	**dódeka**	tho-the-ka				
13	**dekatría**	de-ka-tree-a				
14	**dekatéssera**	the-ka-te-se-ra				
15	**dekapénde**	the-ka-pen-de				
16	**dekaéxi**	the-ka-ek-si				
17	**dekaeptá**	the-ka-ep-ta				
18	**dekaohtó**	the-ka-och-to				
19	**dekaennéa**	the-ka-e-ne-a				
20	**íkosi**	ee-ko-see				
21	**ikosiéna**	ee-ko-see-e-na				